Men-at-Arms • 439

The Canadian Corps in World War I

René Chartrand • Illustrated by Gerry Er

Series editor Martin Windrow

D1208560

DISCARDED
BRADFORD WG
PUBLIC LIBRARY

BRADFORD WG LIBRARY
106 HOLLAND COURT, BOX 130
BRADFORD, ONT. L3Z 2A7

First published in Great Britain in 2007 by Osprey Publishing
Midland House, West Way, Botley, Oxford OX2 0PH, UK
443 Park Avenue South, New York, NY 10016, USA

Email: **info@ospreypublishing.com**

© 2007 Osprey Publishing Ltd.

All rights reserved. Apart from any fair dealing for the purpose of private study,
research, criticism or review, as permitted under the Copyright, Designs and
Patents Act, 1988, no part of this publication may be reproduced, stored in
a retrieval system, or transmitted in any form or by any means, electronic,
electrical, chemical, mechanical, optical, photocopying, recording or otherwise,
without the prior written permission of the copyright owner. Enquiries should
be addressed to the Publishers.

ISBN 978 184603 186 1

Editor: Martin Windrow
Page layouts by Alan Hamp
Typeset in Helvetica Neue and ITC New Baskerville
Index by Glyn Sutcliffe
Originated by PPS Grasmere, Leeds, UK
Printed in China through World Print Ltd.

07 08 09 10 11   10 9 8 7 6 5 4 3 2 1

A CIP catalogue record for this book is available from the British Library

FOR A CATALOGUE OF ALL BOOKS PUBLISHED BY
OSPREY MILITARY AND AVIATION PLEASE CONTACT:

North America:
Osprey Direct, c/o Random House Distribution Center
400 Hahn Road, Westminster MD 21157
Email: **info@ospreydirect.com**

All other regions:
Osprey Direct, UK, PO Box 140, Wellingborough, Northants, NN8 2FA, UK
Email: **info@ospreydirect.co.uk**

Buy online at **www.ospreypublishing.com**

Dedication

To the memory of my great-uncle, Albert Vermette, *22e bataillon
canadien-français*, killed in action 6 August 1916.
Lost but never forgotten.

Author's note

This slim volume attempts to provide a necessarily very concise
account of the background, organization, uniforms, arms and
equipment of the Canadian Corps on the Western Front, with brief
additional notes on other Canadian land, sea and air forces. A list
of units is included, but in the space available it is impossible to list
their actions; that information can be found in other works. There
exist masses of data on this topic, and much that is contained
herein comes from manuscript sources; the bibliography selects
a few, but by no means all of the published sources used.

The author wishes to express his gratitude to Francis Back, the late
Joseph H.Harper, Clive Law, Charles Taylor, the staff at National
Defence's Directorate of History and Heritage, and Library and
Archives Canada in Ottawa.
Unless otherwise credited, all illustrations are from the author's
photographs.

Artist's note

Readers may care to note that the original paintings from which the
colour plates in this book were prepared are available for private
sale. All reproduction copyright whatsoever is retained by the
Publishers. All enquiries should be addressed to:

www.gerryembleton.com

The Publishers regret that they can enter into no correspondence
upon this matter.

**TITLE PAGE Canadian artillery
in action, in a 1918 painting
by Kenneth Forbes. During the
Great War the RCA grew from
a few batteries to large artillery
groups for all five divisions, with
some 20 (mostly field) brigades
and 12 siege batteries, served
by nearly 44,000 men, of whom
2,565 were killed. Canadian
gunners quickly became
proficient and innovative in the
development of artillery barrage
tactics. By 1918 eight Canadian
siege batteries were equipped
with the 6in howitzer shown
here; it could fire a 100lb (45kg)
shell to a distance of 9,500
yards (5.4 miles, 8.7km).
(Canadian War Museum, Ottawa)**

Canadian World War I Statistics

Estimated 1914 population:	7,870,000		Total enlisted in Canadian services:	628,462
Regular army strength in 1914:	3,110			
Total males enlisted in			Canadians in British air services:	c.23,000
Canadian Expeditionary Force:	616,557		Of which, killed or missing:	1,563
Of which, served overseas:	421,510		Canadians in the British Royal Navy:	c.3,000
Military nursing sisters in CEF	2,854		Of which, killed or missing:	c.300
Of which, served overseas:	2,411			
			Total Canadians killed or missing	
Total enlisted in CEF:	619,636		(from Book of Remembrance):	66,655
Of which, killed or missing:	58,990			
Wounded:	149,710		National debt 1914:	$544,000,000
Prisoners of war:	2,820		National debt 1919:	$2,500,000,000
Royal Canadian Navy strength in 1914:	350		Newfoundland population:	230,000
RCN strength in 1918:	5,500		Newfoundlanders enlisted:	12,425
RCN killed or missing:	150		Of which, killed or missing:	1,602

THE CANADIAN CORPS IN WORLD WAR I

INTRODUCTION

Regulars of the Royal Canadian Regt in full dress, c.1913 – from their medals, some are veterans of the Boer War (1900–02). They wear white helmets with scarlet puggaree, brass fittings and regimental badge; scarlet tunics with dark blue collar, cuffs and shoulder straps, white piping and chevrons, brass buttons and collar badges; dark blue trousers with a narrow scarlet stripe, and low black boots, with the brown leather belt of the M1899 Oliver equipment, and Ross rifles. (Private collection)

AS THE 20th CENTURY DAWNED, Canada was a booming country in full development. Enormous on the map, it had only a few million inhabitants spread from the Atlantic to the Pacific, nearly all of them settled within the roughly 200 miles (c.300km) of most easily habitable country north of the continent-wide border with its only neighbour, the United States of America. Since 1885 the transcontinental railway links had opened the Western prairies to settlement, and hundreds of thousands of immigrants had poured in every year; by the early 1900s, cities, towns, farms and ranches were mushrooming between Lake Superior and the Canadian Rockies. Natural resources were being exploited everywhere, and sizeable industries had been founded at Montréal and Toronto, the largest cities.

Politically, most people outside of Canada believed that it was a British 'colony'; in fact, it had attained self-government under the British Crown since the middle of the 19th century, with its own federal parliament. By 1905 the country had nine provinces, each with extensive internal jurisdictions and their own legislatures; apart from this regional aspect, institutions were patterned after those in Britain. Foreign diplomacy was the one area that Canada did not control; this was naturally left to the United Kingdom, the 'mother country' to many Canadians. Canada's diplomatic dealings with the United States mostly concerned mutual trade, and it was (and remains) hard to find more cordial relations between two sovereign nations.

Canada, like its southern neighbour, was (and remains) a country shaped by great waves of immigration. In the 19th century most immigrants came from the British Isles, joined from the turn of the 20th century by many from the Ukraine, Germany and Russia; these mostly settled in the Prairies. Between 1891 and 1911 alone the population rose by nearly three million, to exceed seven million souls.

The diversity of Canada's population had a fundamental impact on its contribution to the Great War; beneath the veneer of Canada's

The 90th CEF Bn (Winnipeg Rifles) on a route march in Canada during the late summer of 1914. All wear the khaki service dress; this was typical of the city units of the Volunteer Militia at that time, though many rural units still had not received it. In the summer heat some men wear only shirts. Most have the rigid Canadian field service cap, but some can be seen to wear Wolseley pattern pith helmets. All carry the Ross rifle. (Private collection)

British-style elite lay some very deep social divisions. In spite of making up 29 per cent of Canada's population, most French-Canadians were often treated as second-class citizens, especially in provinces where they were a minority; some of these had even forbidden French-language schools and courts. English- and Scots-Canadians controlled the federal government's bureaucracy, and the business world presented largely the same picture. In the province of Québec, however, French-Canadians formed about 80 per cent of the population, much of it rural. They fought assimilation with a very high birth rate, and had their own institutions in politics, business and social services, the latter being largely run by the Catholic Church. Because of Québec's weight at the federal ballot box, political compromises were always found and, on the whole, in spite of all the above factors, relations were generally harmonious between Canadians of all origins.

Possibly the one institution that Canadians coast to coast did not care much about before August 1914 was the regular military force. After an acrimonious debate, a Royal Canadian Navy had existed only since 1910; this had a couple of old British cruisers and a few support vessels manned by some 350 officers and men. The regular army – officially called the 'Permanent Force' of the 'Active Militia of Canada' – numbered barely 3,100 officers and men; it consisted of a sole regiment of infantry, three cavalry regiments, and artillery batteries and support units. Fortunately, since 1903 regular cadre corps such as medical, ordnance, signals and so forth had been set up with a small bureaucracy in Ottawa, Canada's capital.

The Royal Military College in Kingston, Ontario, had turned out trained officers since 1876, although it was largely an engineering school. The 'general staff' in Ottawa really consisted only of a few senior administrators. Before August 1914, few Canadian officers had commanded anything more than a few regular companies, and only 12 had completed the British Army's staff course at Camberley in England. In spite of Canada's large French-speaking population, English was the only language used in the armed services. Indeed, youths from French Canada's *bourgeoisie* wishing to enter the Royal Military College were required to be fluent in English – then a rather uncommon accomplishment, and a requirement that amounted to exclusion.

For Canadians attracted to military affairs, the Volunteer Militia – officially given the tongue-twisting name of 'Non-Permanent Active Militia' – was more interesting and, with about 75,000 officers and men in 1914, it was the only sizeable force the country might count upon in an emergency. It had about 110 single-battalion infantry regiments, 35 regiments of cavalry, 40 batteries and 15 companies of artillery, and various support services. It was fairly well organized, and its men were supposed to complete 12 days of training at their area's militia camp every year. Militiamen got a small 'drill' pay; they were issued with basic (and often still scarlet) uniforms, arms and equipment, and might even have access to an armoury building.

Rural units did not fare as well as corps in big cities, which tended to get the cream of the available resources thanks to some of their usually wealthy and influential senior officers. Indeed, politics were a factor in the commissions granted to senior officers; these were usually successful businessmen in their community, looking for the social prestige that the superb pre-1914 officer's full dress uniforms certainly lent them. In practice, apart from its annual training, the only time a militia unit was likely to be called on active duty was in 'Aid to Civil Power', mostly to put down strikes at factories.

There was no obligation to volunteer into the militia, and most young men did not. Still, there were many new cavalry units in the Prairie provinces, joining an already respectable number of volunteers elsewhere – except in the populous province of Québec. There the viable units were mostly made up of English- and Scots-Canadians, with a few well-appointed French-Canadian regiments in Montréal and Québec City, and a host of skeleton rural regiments. The image of a controlling clique of Ontario officers, rumoured to be bigoted Protestants, did not make the institution especially attractive to Francophone potential recruits. For those who nevertheless wished to march and drill, there was a French-speaking para-military alternative: the 'Régiment des Zouaves pontificaux canadiens' (Regiment of Canadian Papal Zouaves), wearing a French-style grey and scarlet uniform with a képi, had the full support of the powerful Catholic clergy. By the early 1900s most large parishes in Québec province had their Zouaves companies.

Because of the Canadian armed forces' anglocentric policies, the potential of French Canada's military manpower was largely ignored. The same exclusions applied to the numerous Catholic Irish-Canadian communities and to Canada's First Nations (Canadian Indians). But then again, most Canadians in early 1914 had many more important things to think about than the militia; none of this really mattered in the least, so long as there was no major international crisis …

A member of the Volunteer Aid Detachments (VAD), trained in nursing care by the Order of St John. The uniform was a grey single-breasted dress with detachable white cuffs and collar, a white apron and small white cap; note the black-and-white armband of the Order. The VADs worked in Canadian and, from 1916, overseas hospitals, in England, France, Italy, Greece and Egypt; by November 1918 the Order had some 400 members from Canada and Newfoundland serving overseas. The Germans twice bombed the Canadian Order's large hospital at Etaples, France, in May 1918, destroying ten wards and killing a nurse, several patients and orderlies and wounding many others. (Private collection)

Six Nations Iroquois Indians enlisted in the 114th (Haldimand) CEF Bn, Ontario, 1916. 'Brock's Rangers' had many Iroquois volunteers and two of its companies were entirely made up of Indians, officers included. They were dispersed among other units in November 1916 when the 114th was broken up to provide reinforcements. About 4,000 Canadian Indians are believed to have served in the CEF; some became snipers, putting their traditional hunting skills to deadly effect (see commentary, Plate E1). (Detail from photo in *Canada in the Great War* ..., Vol.III)

CHRONOLOGY

1914

28 June Archduke Franz Ferdinand of Austria-Hungary is assassinated by a Serbian anarchist in Sarajevo, sparking a series of diplomatic ultimata, general mobilizations, and declarations of war between the Central Powers (Austria-Hungary and Germany) and the Entente (France, Russia and Great Britain). On 4 August Germany invades neutral Belgium, and Great Britain declares war on Germany. Canada, as part of the British Empire, is automatically at war.

3 October Fleet carrying some 33,000 Canadian troops on 31 ships leaves Gaspé for Britain, arriving at Plymouth on 14th – half of Canada's pre-August 1914 total regular and militia force, and at that date by far the largest number of people ever to cross the Atlantic in one fleet. Troops land on 20th and proceed to military camps on Salisbury Plain.

1915

February Troops organized as Canadian Division, under command of MajGen E.Alderson, take over positions on the Western Front in France and Belgium.

24 April Canadian units north-west of St Julien in Ypres Salient of Flanders hold their line despite first German poison gas attacks; Cdn Div suffers 6,036 casualties in Second Battle of Ypres between 15 April and 3 May.

8 May PPCLI, serving with British 27th Div, reduced to 150 effectives in battle of Bellewarde Ridge in south of Ypres Salient.

May–June Cdn Div suffers nearly 3,000 casualties at Festubert and Givenchy.

September 2nd Cdn Div arrives in France, commanded by MajGen R.E.W.Turner, VC; Canadian Army Corps, c.38,000 strong, formed under LtGen E.Alderson, with Canadian MajGen Arthur Currie promoted to command original formation, redesignated 1st Cdn Div. Units previously dispersed under British divisions (e.g. PPCLI, and later Royal Canadian Regt) transferred in.

Winter 1915/16 Canadian Corps holds line in Flanders between Ploegsteert Wood and St Eloi south of Ypres. 3rd Cdn Div (MajGen M.S.Mercer) formed in France.

1916

April 2nd Cdn Div suffers some 1,400 casualties in fighting for St Eloi Craters.

May LtGen Sir Julian Byng succeeds Gen Alderson in command of Canadian Corps.

2–13 June Canadian Corps suffers c.8,000 casualties in Battle of Mont Sorrel, including Gen Mercer killed in 3rd Cdn Div's first action.

1 July Battle of the Somme begins. Newfoundland Regt, with British 29th Div, nearly annihilated in attack on Beaumont Hamel.

August 4th Cdn Div arrives in France. Canadian divisions move from Flanders to the Somme, taking over Australian positions.

15–22 September Battle of Courcelette: 2nd & 3rd Cdn Divs advance behind 'creeping barrage' and with (weak) tank support. Despite some 7,000 casualties they take all objectives and hold them against counter-attacks.

September Canadian Corps strength reaches c.80,000.

26–30 September Further Canadian attacks on Thiepval Ridge make gains but fail to reach the crest.

7–10 October In wet weather, costly Canadian attacks north of Courcelette fail to capture German 'Stuff Trench' positions ('Regina Trench') on the Ancre Heights north-east from Schwaben Redoubt.

11 November 4th Cdn Div, under British II Corps on left of Canadian Corps, finally take Regina Trench.

18 November 4th Cdn Div take all their objectives in final actions of the Battle of the Somme. Division moves to join Canadian Corps on Lens–Arras front at end of month. Total Canadian casualties in three months on the Somme are c.24,000.

1917

February Germans withdraw between Soissons and Arras to prepared shorter front defended in depth – the 'Hindenburg Line'.

9–12 April After two weeks of sophisticated artillery preparation, the four-division Canadian Corps – fighting together for the first time – capture the strategic and supposedly impregnable German positions on Vimy Ridge. The Germans are pushed back 4 miles in some places, and the Corps capture more than 4,000 prisoners and 54 guns. Although the cost is 13,500 killed, missing and wounded, this resounding victory sparks immense pride in Canada and earns great praise from Allied commanders. Four VCs are awarded to Canadian soldiers, and 1st Cdn Div GOC MajGen Currie is knighted.

June Gen Byng takes command of Third Army, and LtGen Sir Arthur Currie succeeds to command of Canadian Corps.

6 July Conscription voted into law in Canada.

August Successful Canadian assault on Hill 70.

CEF nurses are the first Canadian women granted the right to vote; the measure becomes general from September.

October Canadian Corps ordered to Ypres Salient to take part in British offensive – Third Battle of Ypres.

26 October–10 November Battle of Passchendaele: in appalling weather the Canadian Corps take ground in costly attacks, 27th CEF Bn entering the ruins of Passchendaele village first on 6 November. Canadians suffer some 16,000 casualties.

6 December Collision and explosion of the ammunition ship *Mont-Blanc* and the *Imo* in Halifax harbour, the assembly point for convoys sailing to Europe. This catastrophe kills more than 1,600 and injures 9,000, nearly all civilians, and partly levels the city. Nevertheless, convoys are sailing again from Halifax by mid-December.

The very different appearance of Canadian troops on the Western Front, 31 August 1918: these are men of Princess Patricia's Canadian Light Infantry resting at Arras, scene of the first Canadian triumph in the great Allied counter-offensive. Under magnification they can be seen to wear the brass 'CANADA' title at the end of the shoulder straps, above the white-on-red arc-shaped title 'P.P.C.L.I.', above the battalion's 'battle badges' introduced in September 1916 – a semicircle (second battalion in brigade) in green (senior brigade, 7th), over the blue-grey rectangle of 3rd Cdn Division. One man has the regimental badge brazed to the front of his helmet; behind him the stretcher-bearer has no 'P.P.C.L.I.' title and a square battalion patch, presumably for 49th CEF Bn – see Table 1, page 12, and insignia chart, page 44. (Imperial War Museum CO3175)

Sir Samuel Hughes (1853–1921), the vain and self-willed Minister of Militia and Defence at the outbreak of war. A newspaper owner, Volunteer Militia officer and politically powerful member of Parliament, Hughes' character may be read from the fact that he had actually *asked* for the Victoria Cross for his service in South Africa. This was refused, but he did secure a knighthood, and political manoeuvring brought him promotion to general rank. The outbreak of war catapulted Hughes from a relatively minor cabinet post to international stature. He often ignored military planners, the worst case probably being his scrapping of the existing scheme for mobilization, which created massive and unnecessary administrative chaos. His political stance as a passionate Orange Order supremacist did nothing to rally French- and Irish-Canadians to the war effort. His term as minister was both a political and military failure, and increasingly an embarrassment to the Conservative party. Stubborn to the last, he finally had to step down in late 1916. (Print after 'S.B.'; private collection)

1918

21 March–17 July German spring offensives on fronts of British Fifth Army south of Canadian Corps positions around Lens and Vimy (March–April), and of Second Army north of them (April), make spectacular gains, followed by other advances against French fronts further to south (May–July).

29 March Anti-conscription riots break out in Québec City; many killed and wounded when troops open fire on crowds.

April Canadian Corps in various actions during the Battle of the Lys.

27 June Canadian hospital ship *Llandovery Castle* and its lifeboats sunk by a U-boat; nearly all on board perish.

18–20 July Gen Foche launches decisive Franco-American counter-offensive against overextended German armies on the Marne; Allies regain intitiative.

8–11 August Canadian Corps spearheads Allied surprise attacks at Amiens, advancing 12 miles.

26 August–10 November 'Canada's Hundred Days' – the Canadian Corps achieves unbroken advances. Switched north to Arras, the Canadians assault the Hindenburg Line, and pierce it on 2 September. They cross the Canal du Nord on 27 September, take Amiens on 2 October, and capture Cambrai on 12 October. The Germans begin a general withdrawal and the Canadians pursue them, sweeping aside all opposition; they overrun the German defences at Valenciennes on 1 November, and reach Mons on the 10th.

September and October Canadian contingents sent to Russia to aid White armies against Bolsheviks in the Civil War.

11 November Armistice agreed with Germany; end of the Great War.

1919

28 June Treaty of Versailles signed, finalizing terms of German surrender.

October Last Canadian contingents leave Russia.

CANADA IN THE GREAT WAR

When the call to arms was sounded in Canada in August 1914 enthusiasm ran high across the country, and tens of thousands of men volunteered to go to war. The Canadian government offered troops to Britain for overseas service while ordering the mobilization of part of the Volunteer Militia. The idea was to get as many troops over to England as quickly as possible; most were convinced the war would be over in a matter of months.

It was Canada's dubious fortune to have Sir Samuel Hughes as the minister responsible for the Permanent Force and the Volunteer Militia since 1911. A man of great charm, wit and driving energy, allied with consummate political skills, 'Sir Sam' was also a stubborn, pompous racist who would admit no contradiction to his views. As his own son put it, 'God help he who goes against my father's will'. His early plans were to turn the Canadian Militia into something like the Swiss model of battle-ready reserves. This could not be achieved in Canada, a very different society from Switzerland; but Hughes did secure substantial budget increases that brought marked improvements to the Volunteer

Militia. From August 1914 this man of boundless energy, questionable judgement and enormous ego totally dominated Canada's military activity.

During 1911 a plan had been prepared for mobilizing an expeditionary force of one division and a cavalry brigade together with artillery and support units. Its battalions were to be made up from companies called for active duty from various Volunteer Militia regiments and assembled at Camp Petawawa, north of Ottawa. In August 1914, Sir Sam Hughes swept aside this sensible mobilization plan. Instead, he chose to create an entirely new army by forming the Canadian Expeditionary Force (soon known simply as the CEF). All CEF volunteers were directed to assemble at Valcartier, a large new camp being set up near Québec City. This new mobilization scheme created massive administrative problems and confusion; a whole new force was being created that had no direct connection with the existing militia, while needing all its resources and manpower.

The Canadian Expeditionary Force

In August and September tens of thousands of men from militia regiments flocked into Valcartier, to face a wide range of shortages and discomforts in this huge tent city while being organized into new battalions. A CEF battalion had eight companies, each of three officers and 116 enlisted men. Battalions were numbered rather than bearing the traditional titles of long-established militia regiments, but in practice the battalions of the Canadian Division initially sent to Europe were largely made up from members of the pre-war Volunteer Militia. These were the only fairly well-trained, uniformed, equipped and armed men who could be mustered quickly; civilian volunteers were flocking to enlist, but there were not enough supplies to equip them all immediately, and they had to undergo basic training.

Detail from a painting by Richard Jack, 1917, showing a Highlander of the 15th CEF Bn at the Second Battle of Ypres, 22 April–25 May 1915. The 15th was basically the CEF reincarnation of Toronto's 48th Highlanders. He is shown with the khaki Balmoral bonnet, jacket with blue shoulder straps, and kilt of Davidson tartan. (Canadian War Museum, Ottawa)

The new battalions tended to represent specific geographic areas of the country: for instance, the 1st CEF Battalion was raised mainly from 17 militia units in western Ontario, the 2nd from 20 units in eastern Ontario, and the 5th gathered men from seven units in the Western provinces. Some battalions were a near-reincarnation of a militia regiment: for instance, the 3rd CEF had nearly 1,000 men from Toronto's 2nd Queen's Own Rifles; the 9th CEF had over 1,200 men from the 101st Edmonton Fusiliers; the 13th CEF had 1,000 men from Montréal's 5th Royal Highlanders, and 837 of the 15th CEF's 1,283 men came from Toronto's 48th Highlanders.

By September, the first CEF division was being organized in four brigades, each with four battalions – a structure that lasted throughout the war for Canadian divisions. The divisional artillery consisted of two field brigades, each having three six-gun batteries armed with 18-pounders. The divisional cavalry squadron had 196 officers and men drawn from the 19th Alberta Dragoons, and the division had the usual allotment of engineers, ordnance, service and medical corps detachments.

Colour of Princess Patricia's Canadian Light Infantry, 1914–19. Originally intended as a unit HQ flag, it was presented in August 1914 by Princess Patricia of Connaught, daughter of the Governor General of Canada, who designed and embroidered it herself; its crimson field, fringed with gold, had a central blue disc edged gold with a crowned 'PP' cipher in gold. Nicknamed the 'Ric-a-dam-doo' by men of the PPCLI, this became the only unit colour in the whole BEF and CEF that was actually carried with the regiment in battle throughout the war. In February 1919, Princess Patricia further presented the gilded laurel wreath for the pole. It was not an official regimental colour until 1922, when a replica was presented with the King's Colours and was carried until 1934. (From an old tinted print)

There were other troops assembling besides this first CEF division. The Royal Canadian Dragoons and Lord Strathcona's Horse formed – with two mobilized Royal Canadian Horse Artillery batteries – the Canadian Mounted Brigade. Princess Patricia's Canadian Light Infantry, a regiment recruited from British Army veterans living in Canada, was organized at this time under the sponsorship of A.Hamilton Gault, a Montréal businessman.

By mid-September 1914 up to 33,000 men were sent to the port of Gaspé to board a large fleet to be escorted to Britain by Royal Navy warships, sailing on 3 October and arriving at Plymouth, Devon, on 14 October after an uneventful voyage. For their part, the British were somewhat taken aback when faced with finding accommodation for this huge number of men, and it took a while to sort out the inevitable problems. The Canadian troops were finally allowed to land in England on 20 October, and proceeded to Salisbury Plain in Wiltshire, one of the British Army's traditional training areas. Princess Patricia's Canadian Light Infantry ('Princess Pat's') was initially incorporated into the British Army, and was the first Canadian unit to arrive in France in December 1914 as part of the British 29th (Regular) Division. After a rather dreary stay under canvas on Salisbury Plain, the Canadian Division landed in France in February 1915, and moved up the line into the trenches of Flanders.

First blood: Second Ypres, April 1915

All the combatant armies were by now deadlocked in their continuous trench lines, running some 400 miles (650km) south from the beaches of the North Sea to the Swiss border. In the spring of 1915 the Germans produced a new secret weapon to break this deadlock: poison gas. The place selected for its first mass use was at a junction in the Allied line near Ypres, where the 45th (Algerian) and 87th (Territorial) Divs held the French Army's northern flank, adjacent to the southern end of the British Expeditionary Force perimeter; the flank of the BEF's front near St Julien was guarded by the Canadian Division.

On 22 April the Germans released some 160 tons of chlorine gas on what were considered green and unreliable colonial troops. The Algerians were hit first by the strange and sinister yellow-green clouds rolling across No Man's Land; up to 1,400 French troops in the trenches choked and died, more than 2,000 others were disabled, and the survivors broke and fled, opening a four-mile gap in the front. The German infantry did not exploit the unexpected scale of their success fully, and the Canadians counter-attacked to close the gap; their casualties were very high, but this bought time for more troops to come up.

On the night of 23/24 April the Germans launched a more limited gas attack on the Canadians themselves. The fighting was desperate but, though protected only by water-soaked handkerchiefs across their faces and armed with Ross rifles that were prone to jamming, the Canadian Division held the line until reinforcements arrived. This feat established the Canadians' reputation as a very tough fighting force – but at a cost of more than 6,000 dead, missing and wounded. All the Allied troops who survived this first encounter with poison gas were deeply shocked by what they considered a war crime, and felt a furious hunger for revenge. Sir Arthur Currie, later to command the Canadian Corps with such distinction, would recall that the Canadians 'never forgot that gas at the second battle of Ypres, and we never let [the enemy] forget it either. We gassed him on every conceivable occasion, and if we could have killed the whole German army by gas we would gladly have done so'.[1]

From division to corps

Support for the war remained strong in Canada. The 2nd Cdn Div was formed in England during the spring of 1915, and went into the trenches next to the now redesignated 1st Div in September. In December 1915 the 3rd Cdn Div began to form in France and went into the line the following spring, to be joined by the 4th in September 1916. From the time when the 1st Div went to France the Canadian government had been adamant that the battalions it sent to Europe should not be dispersed into other formations of the British Expeditionary Force, and the arrival of the 2nd Div allowed the creation of a small Canadian corps. By October 1916 the Canadian Corps had grown to four infantry divisions supported by strong artillery, cavalry, engineer and auxiliary forces, totalling more than 80,000 men. Command of the Canadian Corps from May 1916 to June 1917 was held by a British general, Sir Julian Byng – one of the few commanders to emerge from the Dardanelles campaign with any credit. A 5th Cdn Div was formed in Britain on 13 February 1917, but remained there, and was broken up in February 1918 to provide reinforcements.

Chaplain G.McL.Dix, 106th CEF Bn (Nova Scotia Rifles), 1916. Chaplains attached to units wore their corps' distinctive cap badge in the shape of a Maltese cross, and their battalion's badge on the lapels. (Private collection)

Internal problems

As 1916 dawned with no end to the carnage in sight, Canada was increasingly divided over the issue of enlistment. The terrible bloodletting on the battlefields of 1915 led to renewed calls for masses of volunteers. In English-speaking Canada many still came forward for the defence of 'King and Country'; but in French Canada the response to the call to arms was far less enthusiastic. Even under the best of circumstances, an appeal made to French-Canadians to come to the defence of France – the mother-country that had abandoned them to the British in 1763 – was likely to receive only a lukewarm reception. From the beginning of the war, the government's policy was to enlist French-Canadians individually and spread them among the various Anglophone CEF battalions, in order to pursue cultural assimilation – an attitude that essentially persisted throughout the war. It was only after a bitter political fight that a single wholly French-Canadian battalion (the famous 22nd, or 'Van-Doos') was authorized in November 1914. Officers' commissions for French-Canadians were rare, and senior rank more so: out of 106 Canadian-born generals, only four were French-Canadians. To add insult to injury, a Presbyterian minister speaking only English was – inexplicably – put in charge of recruitment in the predominantly Catholic and Francophone province of Québec.

French Canada protested through its press and politicians and, most of all, by very low enlistments. To vitriolic accusations in the English-Canadian press of not supporting the war, they replied – unanswerably – that only equal treatment was acceptable for equal sacrifice. The Canadian government's foolish policies thus alienated from the war effort

Table 1: Divisions & Brigades of the Canadian Corps

Canadian Division (from autumn 1915, 1st Division)
1st Brigade: 1st, 2nd, 3rd & 4th Battalions
2nd Bde: 5th, 7th, 8th & 10th Bns
3rd Bde: 13th, 14th, 15th & 16th Bns
4th Bde: 9th, 19th, 11th & 12th Bns
Royal Canadian Artillery : 1st & 2nd Bdes
   Cdn Field Arty
Royal Canadian Engineers: 1st Bde
Royal Canadian Army Service Corps: 1st
   Divisional Train
Canadian Machine Gun Corps: 1st Bn
Canadian Medical Corps: 1st, 2nd & 3rd Field
   Ambulances

2nd Division
4th Bde: 18th, 19th, 20th & 21st Bns
5th Bde: 22nd, 24th, 25th & 26th Bns
6th Bde: 27th, 28th, 29th & 30th Bns
RCA: 5th & 6th Bdes CFA
RCE: 2nd Bde
RCASC: 2nd Div Train
CMGC: 2nd Bn
CMC: 4th, 5th & 6th Fld Ambls

3rd Division
7th Bde: Royal Canadian Regt, PPCLI, 42nd
   & 49th Bns
8th Bde: 1st, 2nd & 3rd Bns Cdn Mounted
   Rifles
9th Bde: 43rd, 52nd, 58th & 116th Bns
RCA: 9th & 10th Bdes CFA
RCE: 3rd Bde
RCASC: 3rd Div Train
CMGC: 3rd Bn
CMC: 8th, 9th & 10th Fld Ambls

4th Division
10th Bde: 44th, 46th, 47th & 50th Bns
11th Bde: 54th, 75th, 87th & 102nd Bns

12th Bde: 38th, 72nd, 78th & 85th Bns
RCA: 3rd & 4th Bdes CFA
RCE: 4th Bde
RCASC: 4th Div Train
CMGC: 4th Bn
CMC: 11th, 12th & 13th Fld Ambls

5th Division (in England)
13th, 14th & 15th Bdes (119th, 125th, 128th,
   134th, 140th, 150th, 156th, 160th, 161st,
   185th & 198th Bns)
RCA: 5th Div Artillery
CMC: 14th Fld Ambl
RCASC: 5th Div Train

Canadian Cavalry Brigade (British 3rd Cav Div)
Royal Canadian Dragoons
Lord Strathcona's Horse
Fort Garry Horse
Royal Canadian Horse Artillery
Machine Gun Squadron
CMC: 7th Fld Ambl

Army and Corps Troops
Canadian Light Horse
RCA: Canadian Corps Horse Artillery; 1st–3rd
   Garrison Artillery
Motor Machine Guns: 1st & 2nd Bdes
Tunnelling Coys: 1st–3rd
Railway Troops: 1st–13th Bns
Labour Troops: HQ; 1st–4th Works Coys
   (plus various small elements e.g. 58th Broad
   Gauge Operating Coy)

In Siberia
16th Bde: 259th & 260th Bns
RCE: 16th Fld Coy
CMGC: 20th Coy
Royal North West Mounted Police: B Sqn

An April 1916 view of Canadian infantry of an unidentified unit 'holding the line' in a trench in the Ypres Salient. This is one of the earliest photos showing Canadian troops wearing the steel helmet issued that March. By that time their dress and arms were mostly the same as those used by their British comrades: many men had British-pattern jackets and greatcoats, SMLE rifles had replaced the Ross, and 08 web equipment the leather Oliver set. Here, the right-hand man wears rubber boots in the mud, and the third man from left has the British sleeveless leather jerkin. (Private collection)

a community representing nearly a third of the national population. As a result, compulsory military service – an unheard-of measure in Canada – was increasingly demanded by the government in order to meet the demand for more men. When conscription was voted in July 1917, French Canada was against it, since apart from those sent to the 22nd CEF Bn the Francophone conscripts would continue to be dispersed between the Anglophone units. The crisis heightened at the end of March 1918, when anti-conscription riots broke out in Québec City and were bloodily put down by troops sent from Toronto. Had the Germans themselves planned to discourage French-Canadian enlistment they could hardly have succeeded better. Nearly a century later, the government's brutally short-sighted handling of this issue is still remembered and resented.

Despite these factors, thousands of French-Canadians still supported the war. Eventually another 14 French-Canadian CEF battalions were raised, but only the 22nd served as a distinct unit on the Western Front, all the others being broken up for reinforcements and posted to other units; as one veteran recalled, it was not uncommon to see a French-Canadian wearing a kilt. An estimated 35,000 French-Canadians enlisted, and of these some 5,900 served in the 22nd – the only ones allowed to use their native French language on service during the war. African-Canadians, although making up only about 9,000 souls, were also often barred from enlisting because of their race, and the 2nd Construction Bn, a labour unit, was deemed the only place for them. Nevertheless, some were seen in the ranks of other CEF battalions.

Although publicly all for the war, some English-Canadians also had their private doubts. When conscription came in 1917 the military authorities were dismayed to find that more demands for exemptions came from Ontario than from Québec. In the end, conscription did not produce the anticipated flock of new recruits and was a failure across the nation. The growth of Canada's war industries, located mainly in Montréal and Toronto, resulted in labour shortages by 1916; consequently tens of thousands of women came into the workforce, but more men were also needed.

Enlistment tended to be relatively low in the Maritime provinces and Québec, the percentages rising as one went further west. This was due to demography as much as to nationalism: there were substantially more men than women in those provinces – some 17 per cent more in Ontario and over 25 per cent more in British Columbia. Another factor was the much higher proportion of enlistment among Canadians born in Britain – some 237,000, or over 38 per cent of the CEF. The proportion of enlistments among the more numerous English-Canadians whose families had been in the country for several generations was lower.

There is no doubt that Canada's contribution could have been greater. In most countries, national armies are a focus of cohesion where the various groups unite for a common cause. In Canada, on the contrary, the military organization actually divided the nation through its refusal to accommodate the culture of the country's largest minority. In spite of all these problems, 'Canada's Answer' to the call to arms during the Great War remains notable. The nation as a whole believed that it was a just war; thus, what was an unmilitary country in August 1914 emerged as a nation with a sizeable and outstandingly successful army by 1918.

(text continues on page 20)

Staff officers with MajGen H.E.Burstall (right), 1916; all wear standard officer's service dress, two with puttees and one with laced field boots – and note that the satchel for the PH anti-gas helmet was carried at all times. At left, displaying red collar tabs and the red/white/red brassard of the Corps staff, is Col Talbot Mercer Papineau. A grandson of Louis-Joseph Papineau, the French-Canadian patriot leader in the 1830s, he encouraged French-Canadians to enlist, arguing in the Québec press that the war was a great international crusade. While agreeing with the noble objectives, his critics — especially his cousin Henri Bourassa, who was the intellectual leader of French Canada — retorted that to be treated with scorn in an army that promoted the cultural assimilation of his own people was no way to fight a war. Colonel Papineau was killed in action on 30 October 1917. (Photo in *Canada in the Great War* ..., Vol.III)

Note: **Bold type** indicates the official designation of a unit; thereafter, any bracketed provincial names in normal type indicate areas of recruitment. The first date quoted for wartime-raised units is the official date of formation. 'England, France' etc indicates 'shipped to England, France' etc in month listed. 'Became' indicates wholesale conversion/redesignation into next-mentioned unit; 'into' indicates 'absorbed/amalgamated into' that unit or units.

Royal Canadian Dragoons Permanent Force (organized 21 Dec 1883); England Oct 1914; France May 1915, served as infantry with 1st Cdn Div until Jan 1916; resumed cavalry role within Cdn Cav Bde and served attached to the British Army; Canada May 1919

Lord Strathcona's Horse (Royal Canadians) Permanent Force (organized 1 July 1901); same services as Royal Canadian Dragoons above

Fort Garry Horse 9 Jan 1916 from Cdn Cav Depot; from 26 Feb 1916, same services as Royal Canadian Dragoons above; disbanded 6 Nov 1920

Special Service Squadron, 19th Alberta Dragoons 6 Aug 1914; to England Oct 1915; France Feb 1915 in 1st Cdn Div; into Cdn Corps Cav Regt 19 May 1916

Squadron of Mounted Rifles 7 Nov 1914; England June 1915; France Sept 1915; First Canadian Hussars (Special Service Sqn) 3 Feb 1916; into Cdn Corps Cav Regt 19 May 1916

3rd 'Overseas' Divisional Squadron 22 Dec 1915; England Jan 1916; France Apr 1916, into Cdn Corps Cav Regt 19 May 1916

Royal Northwest Mounted Police Squadron Apr 1918; England June 1918; France Oct 1918; Canada Mar 1919, demobilized in Regina 14 Mar 1919. 'B' Sqn RNWMP authorized 25 Sept; Vladivostock (Russia) from Nov 1919; disbanded Nov 1920

Canadian Corps Cavalry Regt/Canadian Light Horse Formed France 19 May 1916 as Cdn Corps Cav Regt; Canadian Light Horse 21 Feb 1917; Canada and demobilized Apr 1919

Canadian Cavalry Depot Formed England 24 May 1915; absorbed by Canadian Reserve Cav Regt 5 Apr 1919

Canadian Reserve Cavalry Regt Formed France 20 Feb 1917, amalgamating Cdn reserve cavalry units

1st, 2nd, 3rd Regts, Canadian Mounted Rifles 7 Nov 1914; England June 1915; France Sept 1915; served as infantry until amalgamated to form 1st CMR Bn 1 Jan 1916. (The 1st had a complete mounted pipe band, said to be world's first; no special distinctions except for Royal Stewart tartan pipe bags)

4th, 5th, 6th Regts, Canadian Mounted Rifles 7 Nov 1914; England July 1915; France Oct 1915; served as infantry until amalgamated to form 1st CMR Bn 1 Jan 1916

7th Regt, Canadian Mounted Rifles 7 Nov 1914; England Mar 1915, absorbed by CMR Depot on arrival

8th Regt, Canadian Mounted Rifles 7 Nov 1914; England Oct 1915; provided reinforcements; absorbed into 4th CMR Bn and 39th Reserve Bn, 28–29 Jan 1917

9th Regt, Canadian Mounted Rifles 7 Nov 1914; England Dec 1915; provided reinforcements; absorbed into 5th CMR Bn 29 Jan 1916 and Cdn Cav Depot 3 Feb 1916

10th Regt, Canadian Mounted Rifles 7 Nov 1914; England May 1916; provided reinforcements, into Cdn Cav Depot 22 May 1916

11th Regt, Canadian Mounted Rifles – see 11th CMR Bn below

12th Regt, Canadian Mounted Rifles 7 Nov 1914; England Oct 1915; provided reinforcements, into Cdn Cav Depot 3 Feb 1916

13th Regt, Canadian Mounted Rifles see 13th CMR Bn

1st, 2nd, 4th, 5th Canadian Mounted Rifles Bns Formed France 1 Jan 1916, in 3rd Cdn Div; Canada Mar 1919, demobilized Mar & Apr 1919. (Pipe band in 1st – see above, 1st Regt CMR)

11th Bn, Canadian Mounted Rifles As 11th Regt, 7 Nov 1914; became infantry bn Apr 1916; England July 1916; provided reinforcements; into 24th Reserve Bn (British Columbia), 1 Jan 1917

13th Bn, Canadian Mounted Rifles As 13th Regt, 7 Nov 1914; became infantry bn Apr 1916; England July 1916, absorbed for reinforcements

Depot Regt Overseas Canadian Mounted Rifles 22 Dec 1915; England Oct 1917; disbanded 6 Nov 1920

Royal Canadian Artillery Small Permanent Force (organized 20 Oct 1871) and various volunteer militia batteries mobilized in 1914 grew by 1918 to 37,714 all ranks overseas (9,984 casualties). Mostly deployed on Western Front in 43 field, 9 siege and many other units and sub-units, e.g. howitzer and trench mortar units. Also depot, reserve, ammunition column, and school of gunnery; Canadian Garrison Artillery units served in coast batteries in Canada 1914–19, especially Halifax and Esquimalt; 6th Coy at St Lucia, West Indies, 1917–19.

Royal Canadian Engineers Permanent Force (organized 1 July 1903) and volunteer militia components mobilized in 1914. Served in all theatres.

Royal Canadian Regt Permanent Force (organized 21 Dec 1883); Bermuda Sept 1914, Canada Aug 1915, to England Sept 1915; France Nov 1915, in 3rd Cdn Div; Canada May 1919

Princess Patricia's Canadian Light Infantry 10 Aug 1914; England Oct 1914, in 27th British Div; France Dec 1914, detached to 32nd French Div Jan–Mar 1915, with 3rd Cdn Div from Dec 1915; Canada Mar 1919, became regular Canadian Army Regt 1 Apr 1919. (Pipe band: Hunting Stewart tartan, blue diced Glengarry with blackcock's feathers)

1st Canadian Bn (Ontario Regt) 6 Aug 1914; England Oct 1914; France Feb 1915, in 1st Cdn Div; Canada and demobilized Apr 1919

2nd Canadian Bn (Eastern Ontario Regt) 6 Aug 1914; England Oct 1914; France Feb 1915, in 1st Cdn Div; Canada and demobilized Apr 1919

3rd Canadian Bn (Toronto Regt) 6 Aug 1914; England Oct 1914; France Feb 1915, in 1st Cdn Div; Canada and demobilized Apr 1919

4th (Central Ontario) Bn 6 Aug 1914; England Oct 1914; France Feb 1915, in 1st Cdn Div; Canada and demobilized Apr 1919

5th Bn (Western Cavalry) 6 Aug 1914; England Oct 1914; France Feb 1915, in 1st Cdn Div; Canada and demobilized Apr 1919

6th Bn (Prairie provinces & Northern Ontario) 6 Aug 1914; England Oct 1914, provided reinforcements; into Cdn Cav Depot, Canterbury, 6 Mar 1915

7th Canadian Bn (1st British Columbia) 6 Aug 1914; England Oct 1914; France Feb 1915, in 1st Cdn Div; Canada and demobilized Apr 1919

8th Canadian Infantry Bn (90th Regt) (Manitoba) 6 Aug 1914; England Oct 1914; France Feb 1915, in 1st Cdn Div; Canada Apr 1919, demobilized May

9th Bn 6 Aug 1914; England Oct 1914; became 9th Reserve Bn, 29 Apr 1915; into 9th Reserve Bn (Alberta), 4 Jan 1917

10th Bn (Canadians) (Alberta) 6 Aug 1914; England Oct 1914; France Feb 1915, in 1st Cdn Div; to Canada and demobilized Apr 1919

11th Bn 6 Aug 1914; England Oct 1914; became 9th Reserve Bn, 29 Apr 1915; into 11th Reserve Bn (Manitoba), Jan 1917

12th Bn 6 Aug 1914; England Oct 1914; became 12th Reserve Bn, 29 Apr 1915; into 12th Reserve Bn (Central Ontario), 4 Jan 1917

13th Bn (Royal Highlanders of Canada) (Québec) 6 Aug 1914; England Oct 1914; France Feb 1915, in 1st Cdn Div; Canada and demobilized Apr 1919. (Black Watch & khaki 'Cantlie tartan'; khaki Balmoral/blue Glengarry, red & black dicing; pipe band Royal Stewart)

14th Bn (Royal Montréal Regt) 6 Aug 1914; England Oct 1914; France Feb 1915, in 1st Cdn Div; Canada and demobilized Apr 1919

15th Canadian Bn (48th Highlanders of Canada) (Ontario) 6 Aug 1914; England Oct 1914; France Feb 1915, in 1st Cdn Div; Canada and demobilized Apr 1919. (Davidson tartan; khaki Balmoral/blue Glengarry, red & black dicing; pipe band Stewart of Fingard)

16th Canadian Bn (The Canadian Scottish) (Manitoba) 6 Aug 1914; England Oct 1914; France Feb 1915, in 1st Cdn Div; Canada and demobilized Apr 1919. (Tartan formation: No.1 Coy, Gordon; No.2 Coy, MacKenzie; No.3 Coy, Cameron of Erracht; No.4 Coy, Black Watch. Tartan in England & France: MacKenzie; khaki Balmoral/blue Glengarry, red & white dicing; pipe band red Lennox)

17th Bn 6 Aug 1914; England Oct 1914; became 17th Reserve Bn, 29 Apr 1915; into 17th Reserve Bn (Nova Scotia), 4 Jan 1917. (MacKenzie tartan; blue Glengarry, red & black dicing; pipe band same)

18th (Western Ontario) Canadian Bn 7 Nov 1914; England Apr 1915; France Sep 1915, in 2nd Cdn Div; Canada and demobilized May 1919

19th (Central Ontario) Canadian Bn 7 Nov 1914; England Apr 1915; France Sept 1915, in 2nd Cdn Div; Canada and demobilized May 1919. (Pipe band: Black Watch tartan; blue Glengarry)

20th (Central Ontario) Canadian Bn 7 Nov 1914; England Apr 1915; France Sept 1915, in 2nd Cdn Div; Canada and demobilized May 1919

21st (Eastern Ontario) Canadian Bn 7 Nov 1914; England Apr 1915; France Sept 1915, in 2nd Cdn Div; Canada and demobilized May 1919. (Pipe band: Black Watch tartan; khaki Glengarry with white piping; pipe ribbons & bag MacLeod of Harris)

22nd (French Canadian) Bn (Québec) 7 Nov 1914; England Apr 1915; France Sept 1915, in 2nd Cdn Div; Canada and demobilized May 1919

23rd Bn 21 Oct 1914; England Mar 1915; became 23rd Reserve Bn, 29 Apr 1915; into 23rd Reserve Bn (Québec), Jan 1915

24th Bn (Victoria Rifles) 7 Nov 1914; England Apr 1915; France Sept 1915, in 2nd Cdn Div; Canada and demobilized May 1919

25th Bn (Nova Scotia Rifles) 7 Nov 1914; England Apr 1915; France Sept 1915, in 2nd Cdn Div; Canada and demobilized May 1919. (Pipe band: MacKenzie tartan; blue Glengarry, red & white dicing, blackcock's feather for drummers)

26th (New Brunswick) Bn 7 Nov 1914; England Apr 1915; France Sept 1915, in 2nd Cdn Div; Canada and demobilized May 1919. (Pipe band: MacKenzie tartan; blue Glengarry)

27th (City of Winnipeg) Bn 7 Nov 1914; England May 1915; France Sept 1915, in 2nd Cdn Div; Canada and demobilized May 1919

28th (Northwest) Bn 7 Nov 1914; England June 1915; France Sept 1915, in 2nd Cdn Div; Canada May 1919, demobilized June 1919

29th (Vancouver) Bn 7 Nov 1914; England May 1915; France Sept 1915, in 2nd Cdn Div; Canada and demobilized May 1919. (Pipe band: khaki kilt; blue Glengarry; pipe ribbons & bag MacKinnon tartan)

30th Bn 1 Nov 1914; England Mar 1915; became 30th Reserve Bn, 29 Apr 1915; into 1st Reserve Bn (British Columbia), 4 Jan 1917

31st (Alberta) Bn 7 Nov 1914; England May 1915; France Sept 1915, in 2nd Cdn Div; Canada May 1919, demobilized 1 June 1919

32nd Bn 7 Nov 1914; England Mar 1915; became 32nd Reserve Bn, 2 May 1915; into 15th Reserve Bn (Saskatchewan), 4 Jan 1917

33rd Bn (Ontario) 7 Nov 1914; England Mar 1915; became 33rd Reserve Bn, 7 Apr 1916; into 36th Reserve Bn, 7 Jul 1916

34th Bn (Ontario) 7 Nov 1914; England Oct 1915; became 34th Reserve Bn, 9 Feb 1916; into 36th Reserve Bn, 7 Jul 1916. 34th Bn reorganized 27 Nov 1916 as 34th 'Boys' Bn, disbanded 17 Jul 1917

35th Bn 7 Nov 1914; England Apr 1915; became 35th Reserve Bn, 9 Feb 1916; into 4th Reserve Bn (Western Ontario), 4 Jan 1917. (Pipe band: Davidson tartan; blue Glengarry)

36th Bn 7 Nov 1914; England Jun 1915; became 36th Reserve Bn, 14 Jul 1915; into 3rd Reserve Bn (Central Ontario), 4–6 Jan 1917

37th (Northern Ontario) Bn 7 Nov 1914; England Dec 1915; became 37th Reserve Bn, 27 Jan 1916; into 39th Reserve Bn, 8 Jul 1917

38th (Ottawa) Bn 7 Nov 1914; Bermuda Aug 1915; England May 1916; France June 1916, in 4th Cdn Div; Canada and demobilized June 1919

39th Bn 7 Nov 1914; England July 1915; became 39th Reserve Bn, 19 Jul 1915; into 6th Reserve Bn (Eastern Ontario), 4 Jan 1917

40th (Nova Scotia) Bn 7 Nov 1914; England Oct 1915; became 40th Reserve Bn, 9 Feb 1915; into 26th Reserve Bn, Feb 1917

41st (French-Canadian) Bn (Québec, Eastern Ontario) 7 Nov 1914; England Oct 1915; into 23rd Reserve Bn, 20 Apr 1916

42nd Bn (Royal Highlanders of Canada) (Québec) 7 Nov 1914; England June 1915; France Oct 1915, in 3rd Cdn Div; Canada and demobilized Mar 1919. (Black Watch tartan, incl. pipe band)

43rd Bn (Cameron Highlanders of Canada) (Manitoba) 7 Nov 1914; England June 1915; France Feb 1916, in 3rd Cdn Div; Canada and demobilized Mar 1919. (Cameron of Erracht tartan; khaki Balmoral/blue Glengarry, red & black dicing; pipe band same)

44th (Manitoba) Bn 7 Nov 1914; England Oct 1915; France Aug 1916, in 4th Cdn Div; Canada and demobilized June 1919

45th (Manitoba) Bn 7 Nov 1914; England Mar 1916; became 45th Reserve Bn, 7 Apr 1916; into 11th Reserve Bn, 7 Jul 1916

46th (South Saskatchewan) Bn 7 Nov 1914; England Oct 1915; France Aug 1916, in 4th Cdn Div; Canada and demobilized Jun 1919. (Pipe band: Royal Stewart kilt; blue Glengarry with blackcock's feather)

47th (British Columbia) Bn 7 Nov 1914; England Nov 1915; France Aug 1916, in 4th Cdn Div; Canada and demobilized June 1919

48th (British Columbia) Bn 22 Feb 1915; became 3rd Cdn Pioneer Bn 8 Jan 1916, in 3rd Cdn Div; disbanded May 1917

49th Canadian Bn (Edmonton Regt) 7 Nov 1914; France Oct 1915, in 3rd Cdn Div; Canada and demobilized Mar 1919. (Pipe band: regular uniform but Royal Stewart tartan pipe bags & ribbons. The 49th also had a bear cub mascot)

50th (Calgary) Bn 7 Nov 1914; England Nov 1915; France Aug 1916, in 4th Cdn Div; Canada and demobilized June 1919. (Pipe band: Black Watch tartan)

51st (Edmonton) Bn 7 Nov 1914; England Apr 1915; redesignated The Garrison Duty Bn 13 Nov 1916 and provided reinforcements

52nd (New Ontario) Bn 7 Nov 1914; England Dec 1915; France Feb 1916, in 3rd Cdn Div; Canada and demobilized Mar 1919

53rd (Northern Saskatchewan) Bn 7 Nov 1914; England Apr 1916; broken up for reinforcements July 1916

54th (Kootenay) Bn (British Columbia) 7 Nov 1914; England Nov 1915; France Aug 1916, in 4th Cdn Div; Canada and demobilized June 1919

55th (New Brunswick & Prince Edward Island) Bn 7 Nov 1914; England Oct 1915; became 55th Reserve Bn, 9 Feb 1916; into 40th Reserve Bn, 7 July 1916

56th (Calgary) Bn 7 Nov 1914; England Apr 1916; into 9th Reserve Bn, 7 July 1916

57e Bn (Canadien-Français) (Québec) 20 Apr 1915; England June 1916; broken up for reinforcements to 14th & 22nd Bns July 1916

58th Bn (Ontario) 20 Apr 1915; England Nov 1915; France Feb 1916, in 3rd Cdn Div; Canada and demobilized Mar 1919

59th Bn (Ontario) 20 Apr 1915; England Apr 1916; broken up for reinforcements

60th Canadian Bn (Victoria Rifles of Canada) (Québec) 20 Apr 1915; England Nov 1915; France Feb 1916, in 3rd Cdn Div; absorbed into other units 30 Apr 1917

61st (Winnipeg) Bn 20 Apr 1915; England Apr 1916; broken up for reinforcements

62nd (British Columbia) Bn 20 Apr 1915; England Apr 1916; broken up for reinforcements

63rd (Edmonton) Bn 20 Apr 1915; England Apr 1916; broken up for reinforcements. (Pipe band: blue Glengarry, red & black dicing)

64th Bn (Maritime Provinces) 20 Apr 1915; England Apr 1916; broken up for reinforcements; reorganized 7 Dec 1916, absorbed June & July 1917

65th (Saskatchewan) Bn 20 Apr 1915; England June 1916; broken up for reinforcements

66th Bn (Edmonton Guards) 20 Apr 1915; England June 1916; broken up for reinforcements

67th Bn (Western Scots) 20 Apr 1915; England Aug 1916; broken up for reinforcements 28 Apr 1917. (Pipe band: Douglas tartan kilt; blue Glengarry, red, green & white dicing. Brass band: Douglas tartan trews)

68th (Regina) Bn 20 Apr 1915; England May 1916; broken up for reinforcements

69th French-Canadian Bn (Québec) 10 July 1915; England Apr 1916; broken up for reinforcements

70th Bn (Ontario) 10 July 1915; England Apr 1916; broken up for reinforcements

71st Bn (Ontario) 10 July 1915; England Apr 1916; broken up for reinforcements

72nd Bn (Seaforth Highlanders of Canada) (British Columbia) 10 July 1915; England May 1916; France Aug 1916, in 4th Cdn Div; Canada and demobilized June 1919. (MacKenzie tartan; khaki Balmoral/blue Glengarry, red & black dicing; pipe band same)

73rd Overseas Bn (Royal Highlanders of Canada) (Québec) 10 July 1915; England Apr 1916; France Aug 1916, in 4th Cdn Div; heavy casualties at Vimy & withdrawn from line 14 Apr 1917, absorbed into other units 19 Apr 1917. ('Khaki tartan' kilt – khaki ground with red/green/dark blue stripes; khaki Glengarry with red/green/dark blue stripe around base; khaki Balmoral from July 1916; pipe band same)

74th Bn (Ontario) 10 July 1915; England Apr 1916; broken up for reinforcements 18 July 1916

75th (Mississauga) Bn (Ontario) 10 July 1915; England Apr 1916; France Aug 1916, in 4th Cdn Div; Canada and demobilized June 1919

76th Bn (Ontario) 10 July 1915; England May 1916; broken up for reinforcements July 1916

77th (Ottawa) Bn 10 July 1915; England June 1916; broken up for reinforcements 22 Sept 1916. (Pipe band: khaki Inverness tunic piped white; khaki kilt; khaki Glengarry with two white stripes around band)

78th Bn (Winnipeg Grenadiers) 10 July 1915; England May 1916; France Aug 1916, in 4th Cdn Div; Canada and demobilized June 1919

79th (Manitoba) Bn 10 July 1915; England May 1916; broken up for reinforcements 12 July 1916

80th Bn (Ontario) 10 July 1915; England May 1916; broken up for reinforcements July 1916

81st Bn (Ontario) 10 July 1915; England May 1916; broken up for reinforcements 7 July 1916

82nd Bn (Alberta) 10 July 1915; England May 1916; into 9th Reserve Bn, July 1916. (Pipe band, but had no special distinctions)

83rd Bn (Queen's Own Rifles of Canada) (Ontario) 10 July 1915; England May 1916; into 12th Reserve Bn, 7 July 1916

84th Bn (Ontario) 10 July 1915; England June 1916; broken up for reinforcements July 1916

85th Bn (Nova Scotia Highlanders) 10 July 1915; England Oct 1916; France Feb 1917, in 4th Cdn Div; Canada and demobilized June 1919. (Khaki tartan kilt; khaki Balmoral. Pipe band: Argyll & Sutherland tartan; blue Glengarry, brown turkey fleathers with red centre feather)

86th Bn (Royal Hamilton Light Infantry) 10 July 1915; England Apr 1916; France Aug 1916; into Machine Gun Bn – see Cdn MG Corps, page 19

87th Bn (Canadian Grenadier Guards) (Québec) 22 Dec 1915; England Apr 1916; France Aug 1916, in 4th Cdn Div; Canada and demobilized June 1919

88th Bn (Victoria Fusiliers) (British Columbia) 22 Dec 1915; England June 1916; broken up for reinforcements

89th (Alberta) Bn 22 Dec 1915; England June 1916; broken up for reinforcements

90th Bn (Winnipeg Rifles) 22 Dec 1915; England June 1916; into 11th Reserve Bn, 1 Sept 1917

91st (Elgin) Bn (Ontario) 22 Dec 1915; England June 1916; broken up for reinforcements

92nd Bn (48th Highlanders) (Ontario) 22 Dec 1915; England May 1916; into 5th Reserve Bn, 5 Jan 1917. (Davidson tartan; khaki Balmoral. Pipe band: blue Glengarry. Brass band: khaki Balmoral)

93rd (Peterborough) Bn 22 Dec 1915; England July 1916; into 39th Reserve Bn, 6 Oct 1916

94th (New Ontario) Bn 22 Dec 1915; England July 1916; into 32nd Reserve Bn, 18 July 1916

95th Bn (Ontario) 22 Dec 1915; England June 1916; into 5th Reserve Bn, 5 Jan 1917.

96th Bn (Canadian Highlanders) (Saskatchewan) 22 Dec 1915; England Oct 1916; broken up for reinforcements. (Pipe band: Royal Stewart tartan kilt; pipe bags Black Watch; drummers, Black Watch tartan kilt; green Inverness tunic; black feather bonnet with white-over-red hackle)

97th Bn (American Legion) 22 Dec 1915, recruited mainly from US citizens in Toronto; England Sep 1916; broken up for reinforcements Sept–Oct 1916

98th (Lincoln & Welland) Bn (Ontario) 22 Dec 1915; England July 1916; broken up for reinforcements 15 Oct 1916

99th (Essex) Bn (Ontario) 22 Dec 1915; England June 1916; into 35th Reserve Bn, 7 July 1916

100th Bn (Winnipeg Grenadiers) 22 Dec 1915; England Sept 1916; into 11th Reserve Bn (Manitoba), 20 Jan 1917

101st Bn (Winnipeg Light Infantry) 22 Dec 1915; England July 1916; into 17th Reserve Bn, 16 July 1916

102nd Bn (North British Columbians) 22 Dec 1915; England June 1916; France Aug 1916, in 4th Cdn Div; Canada and demobilized June 1919. (Pipe band: Douglas tartan; blue Glengarry, red, green & white dicing)

103rd Bn (British Columbia) 22 Dec 1915; England July 1916; broken up for reinforcements 13 Nov 1916.

104th Bn (New Brunswick) 22 Dec 1915; England July 1916, in 5th Cdn Div Feb 1917–Feb 1918; into 13th Reserve Bn, Mar 1918.

105th Bn (Prince Edward Island Highlanders) 22 Dec 1915; England July 1916; into 104th Bn, 20 Jan 1917. (No Highland dress)

106th Bn (Nova Scotia Rifles) 22 Dec 1915; England July 1916; into 40th Reserve Bn, 5 Oct 1916

107th (Winnipeg) Bn 22 Dec 1915; became 107th Cdn Pioneer Bn, in France and Flanders from Mar 1917; broken up for reinforcements May 1918. (Pipe band: Argyll & Sutherland tartan kilts for pipers, blue Glengarry with double red & white dicing; drummers, Campbell of Argyll tartan trews, plain blue Glengarry)

108th (Selkirk Manitoba) Bn 22 Dec 1915; England Sep 1916; into 14th Reserve Bn (Manitoba), Jan 1917

109th (Victoria & Haliburton) Bn (Ontario) 22 Dec 1915; England July 1916; into 12th Reserve Bn, 8 Dec 1916

110th (Perth) Bn (Ontario) 22 Dec 1915; England Nov 1916; into 8th Reserve Bn, 2 Jan 1917

111th (South Waterloo) Bn (Ontario) 22 Dec 1915; England Oct 1916; into 35th Reserve Bn, 6 Oct 1916

112th (Nova Scotia) Bn 22 Dec 1915; England July 1916; broken up for reinforcements

113th Bn (Lethbridge Highlanders) (Alberta) 22 Dec 1915; England Oct 1916; into 17th Reserve Bn, 8 Oct 1916. (Pipe band: Argyll & Sutherland tartan; blue Glengarry with blackcock's feather; bass drummer, leopardskin apron)

114th (Haldimand) Bn (Brock's Rangers) (Ontario) 22 Dec 1915; England Oct 1916; into 35th & 36th Reserve Bns, 11 Nov 1916

115th (New Brunswick) Bn 22 Dec 1915; England July 1916; broken up for reinforcements

116th (Ontario County) Bn 22 Dec 1915; England July 1916; France Feb 1917, in 3rd Cdn Div; Canada and demobilized Mar 1919

117th (Eastern Townships) Bn (Québec) 22 Dec 1915; England Aug 1916; reorganized as a Training Bn, and broken up for reinforcements Jan 1917

118th (South Waterloo) Bn (Ontario) 22 Dec 1915; England 6 Feb 1917; into 25th Reserve Bn, 7 Feb 1917

119th (Algoma) Bn (Ontario) 22 Dec 1915; England Aug 1916, in 5th Cdn Div Feb 1917–Feb 1918; into 8th Reserve Bn, 6 Apr 1918

120th (City of Hamilton) Overseas Bn (13th Royal Regiment) 22 Dec 1915; England Aug 1916; broken up for reinforcements

121st Bn (Western Irish) (British Columbia) 22 Dec 1915; England Aug 1916; broken up for reinforcements

122nd (Muskoka) Bn (Ontario) – see Cdn Forestry Corps below

123rd Bn (Royal Grenadiers) (Ontario) 22 Dec 1915; became 123rd Cdn Pioneer Bn, in France and Flanders from Mar 1917; broken up for reinforcements May 1918

124th Bn (Governor General's Body Guard) (Ontario) 22 Dec 1915; became 124th Cdn Pioneer Bn, in France and Flanders from Mar 1917; broken up for reinforcements May 1918

125th Bn (1st Overseas Bn of 38th Regt Dufferin Rifles) (Ontario) 22 Dec 1915; England Aug 1916, in 5th Cdn Div Feb 1917–Feb 1918; broken up for reinforcements

126th (Peel) Bn (Ontario) 22 Dec 1915; England Aug 1916; into 109th & 116th Bns, 15 Oct 1916

127th (12th Regt York Rangers) (Ontario) 22 Dec 1915; England Aug 1916; France, as 2nd Bn Cdn Railway Troops, June 1917

128th (Moose Jaw) Bn (Saskatchewan) 22 Dec 1915; England Aug 1916, in 5th Cdn Div Feb 1917–Feb 1918; broken up for reinforcements

129th (Wentworth) Bn (Ontario) 22 Dec 1915; England Aug 1916; broken up for reinforcements

130th (Lanark & Renfrew) Bn (Ontario) 22 Dec 1915; England Oct 1916; into 12th Reserve Bn, 6 Oct 1916

131st (Westminster) Bn (British Columbia) 22 Dec 1915; England Nov 1916; broken up for reinforcements

132nd (North Shore New Brunswick) Bn 22 Dec 1915; England Nov 1916; broken up for reinforcements

133rd Bn (Norfolk's Own) (Ontario) 22 Dec 1915; England Nov 1916; into 3rd Reserve Bn, 4–6 Jan 1917

134th (48th Highlanders) Bn (Ontario) 1 Dec 1916; England Aug 1916; into 12th Reserve Bn, 7 Mar 1918. (Pipe band: Davidson tartan; blue Glengarry with blackcock's feathers)

135th (Middlesex) Bn (Ontario) 22 Dec 1915; England Aug 1916; broken up for reinforcements 15 Oct 1916

136th (Durham) Bn (Ontario) 22 Dec 1915; England Oct 1916; into 39th Reserve Bn, 6 Oct 1916

137th (Calgary) Bn 22 Dec 1915; England Aug 1916; into 21st Reserve Bn (Alberta), 10 Jan 1917

138th (Edmonton, Alberta) Bn 22 Dec 1915; England Aug 1916; into other bns Oct & Dec 1916

139th (Northumberland) Bn (Ontario) 22 Dec 1915; England Oct 1916; into 36th Reserve Bn, 5 Oct 1916

140th Bn (New Brunswick) 22 Dec 1915; England Oct 1916; into 13th Reserve Bn, 27 Jan 1917

141st (Rainy River District) Bn (Border Bull Moose) (Ontario) 22 Dec 1915; England May 1917; into 18th Reserve Bn, 7 May 1917

142nd Bn (London's Own) (Ontario) 22 Dec 1915; England Nov 1916; into 23rd Reserve Bn, 12 Nov 1916

143rd Bn (British Columbia Bantams) – became 143rd Railway Construction Bn – see Canadian Railway Troops, page 19

144th (Winnipeg Rifles) 22 Dec 1915; England Sept 1916; broken up for reinforcements Nov 1916

145th (New Brunswick) Bn 22 Dec 1915; England Oct 1916; into 9th Reserve Bn, 7 Oct 1916

146th Bn (Ontario) 22 Dec 1915; England Oct 1916; into 95th Bn, 6 Oct 1916

147th (Grey) Bn 22 Dec 1915; England Nov 1916; into 8th Reserve Bn (Central Ontario), 20 Jan 1917

148th Bn (Ontario) 22 Dec 1915; England Oct 1916; into 20th Reserve Bn (Québec), 8 Jan 1917

149th Bn (Lambtons) (Ontario) 22 Dec 1915; England Apr 1917; into 25th Reserve Bn, 18 Apr 1917

150th Bn (Carabiniers Mont-Royal) (Québec) 22 Dec 1915; England Oct 1916, in 5th Cdn Div Feb 1917–Feb 1918; into 10th Reserve Bn, 3 Mar 1918

151st (Central Alberta) Bn 22 Dec 1915; England Oct 1916; into 9th and 11th Reserve Bns, 13 Oct 1916

152nd (Weyburn-Estevan) Bn (Saskatchewan) 22 Dec 1915; England Oct 1916; into 32nd Reserve Bn, 21 Oct 1916

153rd (Wellington) Bn (Ontario) 22 Dec 1915; England Oct 1916; into 25th Reserve Bn, 7 May 1917

154th (Stormont-Dundas-Glengarry) Bn 22 Dec 1915; England Oct 1916; into 6th Reserve Bn (Eastern Ontario), 4 Jan 1917. (Highland uniform approved but not worn. Pipe band: khaki tartan; khaki Inverness tunic piped white, khaki Glengarry with two stripes around band, Cameron tartan pipe bags)

155th (Quinte) Bn 22 Dec 1915; England Oct 1916; into 6th Reserve Bn (Eastern Ontario), 4 Jan 1917

156th (Leeds & Grenville) Bn (Ontario) 22 Dec 1915; England Oct 1916; broken up for reinforcements 1 Nov 1916; reconstituted 27 Dec 1916, in 5th Cdn Div in England Feb 1917–Feb 1918; broken up for reinforcements Mar 1918

157th (Simcoe Foresters) (Ontario) 22 Dec 1915; England Oct 1916; into 116th & 125th Bns, 8 Dec 1916

158th Bn (The Duke of Connaught's Own) 22 Dec 1915; England Nov 1916; into 1st Reserve Bn (British Columbia), 4 Jan 1917

159th Bn (1st Algonquins) 22 Dec 1915; England Nov 1916; into 8th Reserve Bn (Central Ontario), 2 Jan 1917

160th (Bruce) Bn (Ontario) 22 Dec 1915; England Oct 1916, in 5th Cdn Div Feb 1917–Feb 1918; into 4th Reserve Bn, 23 Feb 1918

161st (Huron) Bn (Ontario) 22 Dec 1915; England Nov 1916, in 5th Cdn Div Feb 1917–Feb 1918; into 4th Reserve Bn, 23 Feb 1918

162nd (Parry Sound) Bn (Ontario) 22 Dec 1915; England Nov 1916; into several Reserve bns Jan 1917

163rd Bn (French-Canadian) 22 Dec 1915; Bermuda May 1916; England Nov–Dec 1916; into 10th Reserve Bn (Québec), 4–6 Jan 1917

164th (Halton and Dufferin) Bn (Ontario) 22 Dec 1915; England Apr 1917, in 5th Cdn Div June 1917–Feb 1918; into 8th Reserve Bn, 16 Apr 1918

165th Bn (Acadiens) (New Brunswick) 22 Dec 1915; England Apr 1917; into 13th Reserve Bn, 14 Apr 1917

166th Bn (Queen's Own Rifles of Canada) 22 Dec 1915; England Oct 1916; into 12th Reserve Bn (Central Ontario), 4 Jan 1917

167th (Canadien-Français) Bn 22 Dec 1915; England Dec 1916; became Québec Recruiting Depot, 15 Jan 1917, providing reinforcements mainly to 22nd Bn

168th Bn (Oxfords) (Ontario) 22 Dec 1915; England Nov 1916; into several Reserve bns from Dec 1916. (Pipe band: Hunting Stewart tartan; blue Glengarry)

169th Bn (109th Regt) 15 July 1916; England Oct 1916; into 5th Reserve Bn (Central Ontario), 4 Jan 1917

170th Bn (Mississauga Horse) (Ontario) 15 July 1916; England Oct 1916; into 169th Bn, 8 Dec 1916

171st Bn (Québec Rifles) 15 July 1916; England Nov 1916; into 20th Reserve Bn (Québec), 8 Jan 1916

172nd Bn (Rocky Mountain Rangers) 15 July 1916; England Oct 1916; into 24th Reserve Bn (British Columbia), 1 Jan 1917

173rd Bn (Canadian Highlanders) 15 July 1916; England Nov 1916; into 2nd Reserve Bn (Central Ontario), 20 Jan 1917. (Argyll & Sutherland tartan; khaki Balmoral. Pipe band: blue Glengarry with blackcock's feathers)

174th Bn (Cameron Highlanders of Canada) (Manitoba, Saskatchewan) 15 July 1916; England May 1917; into 14th Reserve Bn, 7 May 1917. (Cameron of Erracht tartan. Pipe band: blue Glengarry with long black feather)

175th (Medicine Hat) Bn 15 July 1916; England Oct 1916; into 21st Reserve Bn (Alberta), 20 Jan 1917

176th Bn (Niagara Rangers) (Ontario) 15 July 1916; England May 1917; into 12th Reserve Bn, 9 May 1917

177th Bn (Simcoe Foresters) (Ontario) 15 July 1916; England May 1917; into 3rd Reserve Bn, 14 May 1917

178th (Canadien-Français) Bn (Québec) 15 July 1916; England Mar 1917; into 10th Reserve Bn, 19 Mar 1917

179th Bn (Cameron Highlanders of Canada) 15 July 1916; England Oct 1916; into 14th Reserve Bn (Manitoba), 4–10 Jan 1917. (Cameron of Erracht tartan; khaki Balmoral. Pipe band: blue Glengarry with red & black dicing)

180th Bn (Sportsmen) (Ontario) 15 July 1916; England Nov 1916; into 3rd Reserve Bn (Central Ontario), 4–6 Jan 1917

181st (Brandon) Bn (Manitoba) 15 July 1916; England Apr 1917; into 18th Reserve Bn, 30 Apr 1917

182nd (Ontario) Bn 15 July 1916; England May 1917; into 3rd Reserve Bn, 17 May 1917

183rd Bn (Manitoba Beavers) 15 July 1916; England Oct 1916; broken up for reinforcements 1 Nov 1916

184th Bn (Manitoba) 15 July 1916; England Nov 1916; into 11th Reserve Bn, 12 Nov 1916

185th Canadian Infantry Bn (Cape Breton Highlanders) (Nova Scotia) 22 Dec 1915; England Oct 1916, in 5th Cdn Div Feb 1917–Feb 1918; into 17th Reserve Bn, Feb–Mar 1918. (Pipe band: Argyll & Sutherland tartan; blue Glengarry with two brown cock's feathers and green central feather)

186th (Kent) Bn (Ontario) 15 July 1916; England Apr 1917; into 4th Reserve Bn, 19 Apr 1917

187th (Central Alberta) Bn 15 July 1916; England Dec 1916; into 21st Reserve Bn (Alberta), Jan–Feb 1917

188th (Saskatchewan) Bn 15 July 1916; England Oct 1916; into 15th Reserve Bn (Saskatchewan), 20 Jan 1917

189th (Canadien-Français) Bn (Québec) 15 July 1916; England Oct 1916; into 69th Bn, 6 Oct 1916

190th Bn (Winnipeg Rifles) 15 July 1916; England May 1917; into 18th Reserve Bn, 14 May 1917

191st (Southern Alberta) Bn 15 July 1916; England Apr 1917; into 21st Reserve Bn, Apr & June 1917

192nd (Crow's Nest Pass) Bn (Alberta) 15 July 1916; England Nov 1916; into 9th Reserve Bn, 16 Nov 1916

193rd Bn (Nova Scotia Highlanders) 15 July 1916; England Oct 1916; into 17th Reserve Bn (Nova Scotia), 23 Jan 1917. (Khaki tartan; khaki Balmoral. Pipe band: Argyll & Sutherland tartan; blue Glengarry with brown turkey feathers with red central feather)

194th (Edmonton Highlanders) 15 July 1916; England Nov 1916; into 9th Reserve Bn (Alberta), 4 Jan 1917. (Pipe band: khaki, later Black Watch tartan; blue Glengarry with blackcock's feathers)

195th (City of Regina) Bn 15 July 1916; England Nov 1916; into 32nd Reserve Bn, 11 Nov 1916

196th (Western Universities) 15 July 1916; England Nov 1916; into 19th Reserve Bn (Saskatchewan), 2 Jan 1917

197th Bn (Vikings of Canada) (Western Canada) 15 July 1916; England Feb 1917; into 11th Reserve Bn, 7 Feb 1917

198th Bn (Canadian Buffs) (Ontario) 15 July 1916; England Apr 1917, in 5th Cdn Div May 1917–Feb 1918; into 3rd Reserve Bn, 7 Mar 1918

199th Bn Duchess of Connaught's Own Irish Canadian Rangers (Québec) 15 July 1916; England Dec 1916, in 5th Cdn Div Feb 1917–May 1917; into 23rd Reserve Bn (Duchess of Connaught's Own Irish Canadian Rangers), 11 May 1917

200th (Winnipeg) Bn 15 July 1916; England May 1917; into 11th Reserve Bn, 15 May 1917

201st Bn (Toronto Light Infantry) 15 July 1916; recruited only two coys, absorbed in Canada by 170th & 198th Bns, 25 Sep 1916

202nd (Sportman's) Bn (Alberta) 15 July 1916; England Nov 1916, in 5th Cdn Div 13 Feb–27 May 1917, when into 9th Reserve Bn

203rd Bn (Winnipeg Rifles) 15 July 1916; England Nov 1916; into 18th Reserve Bn (Manitoba), 12 Jan 1917

204th Bn (Beavers) (Ontario) 15 July 1916; England Apr 1917; into 2nd Reserve Bn, 8 Apr 1917

205th (Hamilton) Bn 15 July 1915; into Cdn MG Depot in Canada, 20 Dec 1916

206th (Canadien–Français) Bn (Québec) 15 July 1916; sent two drafts to reinforce 163rd Bn in Bermuda, July and Aug 1916; remaining personnel into 167th Bn, 17 Aug 1916

207th (Ottawa-Carleton) Bn 15 July 1916; England June 1917; into 7th Reserve Bn, 14 June 1917

208th Bn (Canadian Irish) (Ontario) 15 July 1916; England May 1917, in 5th Cdn Div; into 2nd & 8th Reserve Bns, Feb 1918

209th (Swift Current) Bn (Saskatchewan) 15 July 1916; England Nov 1916; into 9th Reserve Bn (Alberta), 4 Jan 1917

210th Bn (Frontiersmen, Western Canada) 15 July 1916; England Apr 1917; into 19th Reserve Bn, 6–10 May 1917

211th Bn (American Legion) 15 July 1916; recruited mainly from US citizens in British Columbia & Alberta; England Dec 1916; into 26th Reserve Bn (Nova Scotia), Jan–Feb 1917

212th Bn (American Legion) 15 July 1916; recruited mainly from US citizens in Manitoba & Saskatchewan; into 97th Bn in Canada, Jan–Feb 1917

213th Bn (American Legion) 15 July 1916; recruited mainly from US citizens in Ontario, Québec & the Maritime Provinces; part to England, Sept 1916, as reinforcements; reorganized as Draft Giving Depot Bn, 7 Nov 1916

214th (Saskatchewan) Bn 15 July 1916; England Apr 1917; into 15th Reserve Bn, 10 May 1917

215th Bn (2nd Overseas Bn of 38th Regiment Dufferin Rifles) (Ontario) 15 July 1916; England May 1917; into 2nd Reserve Bn, 10 May 1917

216th Overseas Bn (Bantams) 15 July 1916; England Apr 1917; into 3rd Reserve Bn, 5 & 14 May 1917

217th (Qu'Appelle) Bn 15 July 1916; England 29 Sep 1916; into 19th Reserve Bn, 10 June 1917

218th (Edmonton) Bn 15 July 1915; England & France 1916; into 8th Cdn Railway Construction Bn, 15 June 1917

219th Highland Bn (Nova Scotia) 15 July 1916; England Oct 1916; into 17th Reserve Bn (Nova Scotia), 23 Jan 1917. (Khaki tartan; khaki Balmoral. Pipe band: Argyll & Sutherland tartan; blue Glengarry with brown turkey feathers with red central feather. Brass band: blue Glengarry with white & red dicing)

220th Bn (12th Regt York Rangers) (Ontario) 15 July 1916; England May 1917; into 3rd Reserve Bn, 7 May 1917

221st Bn (Manitoba) 15 July 1916; England Apr 1917; into 11th Reserve Bn, 30 Apr 1917

222nd Bn 15 July 1916; England Nov 1916; into 19th Reserve Bn (Saskatchewan), 2 Jan 1917

223rd Bn (Canadian Scandinavians) (Western Canada) 15 July 1916; England May 1917; into 11th Reserve Bn, 15 May 1917

224th Bn (Ottawa) 15 July 1916; England 1917; into Cdn Forestry Corps, Mar 1917. (Pipe band: MacDougall tartan; blue Glengarry with blackcock's feathers)

225th (Kootenay) Bn (British Columbia) 15 July 1916; England Feb 1917; into 16th Reserve Bn, 7 Feb 1917

226th Bn (Men of the North) 15 July 1916; England Dec 1916; into 14th Reserve Bn (Manitoba), 4–10 Jan 1917

227th (Sudbury-Manitoulin-Algoma) Bn (Men o' the North) (Ontario) 15 July 1916; England Apr 1917; into 8th Reserve Bn, 22 Apr 1917

228th Bn (Northern Fusiliers) (Ontario) 15 July 1916; England & France 1917; into 6th Bn, Cdn Railway Troops 15 June 1917. (Pipe band: Davidson tartan; blue Glengarry)

229th (South Saskatchewan) Bn 15 July 1916; England Apr 1917; into 19th Reserve Bn, 10 May 1917

230th Bn (Voltigeurs Canadiens-Français) (Québec) 15 July 1916; England Mar 1917; into Cdn Forestry Corps Mar 1917

231st Bn (Seaforth Highlanders of Canada) (British Columbia) 15 July 1916; England Apr 1917; into 24th Reserve Bn, Apr–May 1917. (Pipe band: MacKenzie tartan; khaki Balmoral)

232nd (Saskatchewan) Bn 15 July 1916; England Apr & June 1917; into 15th Reserve Bn, Apr–June 1917

233rd Bn (Canadiens-Français du Nord-Ouest) (Western Canada) 15 July 1916; into 178th Bn in Canada, 3 Mar 1917

234th (Peel) Bn (Ontario) 15 July 1916; England Apr 1917; into 12th Reserve Bn, 1 May 1917

235th Bn (Ontario) 15 July 1916; England May 1917; into 3rd Reserve Bn, 14 May 1917

236th Bn (New Brunswick Kilties) 15 July 1916; redesignated (Maclean Highlanders) 15 Oct 1917; England Nov 1917; into 20th Reserve Bn, 13 Mar 1918. (Red Dress MacLean tartan; khaki Balmoral with black feathers tipped white. Pipe band: blue Glengarry with blackcock's feathers)

237th Bn (American Legion) 15 July 1916; recruited mainly from US citizens in Québec, New Brunswick, Nova Scotia & Prince Edward Island; into 97th Bn, 18 Sept 1916

238th Bn (Québec) 15 July 1916; France, into Cdn Forestry Corps, 17 July 1917

239th Bn (Nova Scotia) 15 July 1916; England 1917; into 3rd Bn, Cdn Railway Troops, 15 June 1917

240th Bn (Ontario) 15 July 1916; England May 1917; into 7th Reserve Bn, 17 May 1917

241st Bn (Canadian Scottish Borderers) (Ontario) 15 July 1916; England May 1917; into 5th Reserve Bn, 9 May 1917. (Khaki tartan; blue diced Glengarry. Pipers: MacGregor tartan; blue diced Glengarry with blackcock's feather)

242nd Bn (Québec) 15 July 1916; France, into Cdn Forestry Corps, 17 July 1917. (Pipe band: Ferguson tartan; blue Glengarry with blackcock's feather)

243rd Bn (Saskatchewan) 15 July 1916; England June 1917; into 15th Reserve Bn, 10 June 1917

244th Bn (Kitchener's Own) (Québec) 15 July 1916; England Apr 1917; into 23rd Reserve Bn, 28 Apr 1917

245th Bn (Canadian Grenadier Guards) (Québec) 15 July 1916; England May 1917; into 23rd Reserve Bn, 25 May 1917

246th Infantry Bn (Nova Scotia) 14 July 1916; England June 1917; into 17th Reserve Bn & 185th Bn, 10-12 June 1917. (MacKenzie tartan; khaki Balmoral. Pipers: blue diced Glengarry with blackcock's feathers)

247th (Victoria & Haliburton) Bn (Ontario) 1 May 1917; understrength, into 235th Bn in Canada, 1 Apr 1917

248th Bn (Ontario) 1 May 1917; England June 1917; into 8th Reserve Bn, 10 June 1917

249th (Saskatchewan) Bn 1 May 1917; England Mar 1918; into 15th Reserve Bn, 4 Mar 1918

250th (Winnipeg) Bn 1 May 1917; into 249th Bn in Canada, 10 Oct 1917

251st Bn (Good Fellows) (Manitoba) 1 May 1917; England Oct 1917; into 18th Reserve Bn, 18 Oct 1917

252nd (Lindsay) Bn (Ontario) 1 May 1917; England June 1917; into 6th Reserve Bn, 12 June 1917

253rd (Queen's University) Highland Bn 1 May 1917; recruited throughout Canada from university students; England May 1917; into 5th Reserve Bn, 9 May 1917. (Pipe band: Argyll & Sutherland tartan; Balmoral with grey & red turkey feathers)

254th Bn (Quinte's Own) (Ontario) 1 May 1917; England June 1917; into 6th Reserve Bn, 10 June 1917

255th Bn (Queen's Own Rifles of Canada) (Ontario) 1 May 1917; England June 1917; into 12th Reserve Bn, 10 June 1917

256th Bn (Toronto) 1917; England, into 10th Bn, Cdn Railway Troops, 15 June 1917

257th Bn (Ottawa) 1917; England, into 7th Bn, Cdn Railway Troops, 15 June 1917

258th (Canadien-Français) Bn (Québec) 1 May 1917; into 10th Reserve Bn, 1 Nov 1917

259th Bn (Canadian Rifles) (Ontario & Québec) 1 Nov 1918; served in Siberia, Jan–May 1919; demobilized at Victoria, 1 June 1919

260th Bn (Canadian Rifles) (New Brunswick, Nova Scotia, Prairie Provinces & British Columbia) 1 Nov 1918; served in Siberia, Jan–May 1919; demobilized at Victoria, 22 May 1919

Canadian Machine Gun Corps 15 Sep 1914; grew to 4 bns, 19 coys and sections in nearly all infantry bns in Canadian Corps.

Canadian Tank Bns Formed in France: 1st Bn, 1 July 1918; 2nd Bn, 15 Oct 1918; 3rd Bn, 29 Nov 1918

Canadian Labour (or Construction) Bns 4 bns, formed 1916, France & Flanders; 1st & 4th Bns into Engineers, 2nd attached to Forestry Corps (see below), 3rd into Railway Troops, 1917

2nd Construction Bn Raised in Nova Scotia from 5 July 1916, this first and only African-Canadian battalion had white officers except for the chaplain, Rev William A.White – the first African-Canadian to hold an officer's commission in the Canadian Armed Forces. England Apr 1917, and redesignated Construction Coy; France May 1917; attached to No.5 District, Cdn Forestry Corps; to Nova Scotia Regimental Depot at Brampton, UK, Dec 1918; to Halifax Jan 1919.

Canadian Railway Troops Originated as Canadian Overseas Railway Construction Corps, formed early 1915 with 540 volunteers of Canadian Pacific Railway; proved very useful; 6 Railway Construction companies raised Feb 1917, and 14 numbered bns 15 June 1917; additional specialist companies brought strength to 12,000 men. Built nearly 2,573 miles of track and operated most railways of the British forces in France.

Canadian Pioneer Bns 1st & 2nd Bns formed 22 Dec 1915; 3rd, 4th & 5th, 15 July 1916. Served France and Flanders; into Royal Canadian Engineers, Mar 1918. See also 109th, 123rd & 124th Bns. (Pipe band of 1st Pioneer Bn: Mackenzie tartan; khaki Balmoral)

Canadian Corps Cyclist Bn Formed in France 12 May 1916 from Divisional Cyclist Companies; Canada and demobilized May 1919

Canadian Forestry Corps Initially the 224th, 238th & 242nd Bns absorbed into this corps of skilled lumbermen in summer 1916. Eventually had 7 bns and 101 coys and depots in England and France in 1917–18.

Canadian Military Police Corps 13 detachments from 15 Oct 1917; two served with Canadian Corps in France

1st Canadian Bridging Coy Formed in France from railway bns Sept 1918; Palestine & Syria Oct 1918; England Feb 1919, to railway bns depot

Canadian Army Medical Corps Permanent Force (organized 2 July 1904), grew to 1,351 medical officers, 1,886 nurses & 12,243 field medics and orderlies. Served in England, France, Flanders, Greece, Dardanelles, Egypt, Palestine, Mesopotamia (Iraq) and Russia

Canadian Army Veterinary Corps Permanent Force (organized 1910)

Canadian Army Dental Corps Formed 15 Aug 1915, grew to some 1,500 personnel serving in England, France, Greece and Egypt

Canadian Army Service Corps Permanent Force (organized 1 Dec 1903)

Canadian Army Ordnance Corps Permanent Force (organized 1 July 1903)

Canadian Army Pay Corps Permanent Force (organized 1 Dec 1906)

Corps of Military Staff Clerks Permanent Force (organized 1 Sept 1905)

Canadian School of Musketry Corps Permanent Force (organized 15 Apr 1914)

Corps of Guides Intelligence units (organized 1 Apr 1903)

Canadian Signal Corps Permanent Force (organized 24 Oct 1903)

Canadian Chaplain Services Grew to 426 chaplains during the war, in England and France

Reserve Battalions 36 numbered bns formed in England from late 1916, to amalgamate new CEF bns to reinforce Canadian Corps in France; into Territorial Regts, Apr 1918

Depot Bns Formed in Canada in 1917; into Territorial Regts, Apr 1918

Territorial Regts Formed in England 15 Apr 1918, incorporating Reserve and Depot bns under provincial titles e.g. '1st Québec Regiment'

Militia Drafts Temporary units attached to Volunteer Militia units formed in Canada from June 1917, to incorporate drafts sent overseas. Usually named after the Volunteer Militia unit it was attached to, e.g. '56th Grenville Regiment (Lisgar Rifles) Overseas Draft'

Canadian Volunteer Militia in Canada 36 cavalry, 107 infantry and rifle regts (3 more formed from Sept 1914), 705 Cadet companies, with Volunteer Militia components to artillery, engineers, guides and service corps listed above.

LtGen Sir Julian Byng, the British commander of the Canadian Corps from September 1916 to June 1917. In a few months this confident and innovative general transformed the exhausted Canadian divisions on the Somme into a remarkable assault force; he had an outstanding eye for detail, while keeping a clear grasp of strategic objectives. Caring and approachable, he was well liked by Canadians, and 'Byng of Vimy' became Governor General of Canada after the war. (Private collection)

CORPS OPERATIONS

To the hundreds of thousands of men overseas and in the trenches, the divisive problems at home were a world away. They were set on defeating the enemy and, by 1917, the Canadian Corps deployed on the Western Front formed a tough, disciplined and battle-hardened formation. This was due in no small measure to the rising professionalism of some of the senior Canadian officers. The Englishman Sir Julian Byng was the corps commander and, to his everlasting credit, he had the wisdom to seek out and give responsibility to the more gifted Canadian commanders.

The most remarkable of these was Arthur Currie. A businessman from British Columbia who had also been a militia officer before the war, Currie revealed himself to be an outstanding tactician, and was promoted rapidly, despite the opposition of Minister of Militia, Sir Sam Hughes. By 1917, Currie was commanding the 1st Cdn Div and had the high esteem of the senior commanders of the BEF for his outstanding and intelligent battle planning. There were many other excellent Canadian officers, such as H.E.Burstall, commanding the 2nd Cdn Div from December 1916, and artillery commander A.L.McNaughton. One of the great strengths of the Canadian Corps was its highly integrated and flexible organization compared to other armies: its various elements could be changed and reinforced on the spot. As Currie put it, there was 'no use in waiting until the end of the war to make necessary changes'.

Vimy Ridge

On 9 April 1917, Easter Monday, the Canadian Corps attacked the previously impregnable German positions at Vimy Ridge. By mid-afternoon the initial objectives had been taken, with some 4,000 German prisoners, and its supporting works fell within three days. This meticulously planned assault was the biggest single advance made on the Western Front since the beginning of the war, and (by Western Front standards) with relatively low casualties: 13,500 men, including 2,500 killed. The significance of Vimy Ridge for Canadians, however, was far greater than a single battlefield victory. For the first time in Canada's history, a large Canadian formation had attacked as a national unit and had achieved a rousing victory. In spite of all the political and social divisions at home, Vimy had an extraordinary effect on the national psyche: Canadians gradually moved away from seeing themselves as citizens from a self-governing British dominion, and towards a consciousness of being proud citizens of a fully independent nation. Vimy Ridge was now celebrated as Canada's coming-of-age as a country. On 8 June MajGen Arthur Currie was knighted on the battlefield of Vimy by his Sovereign, King George V, and succeeded Sir Julian Byng as commander of the CEF.

Passchendaele

Sir Douglas Haig assigned the Canadian Corps to the attack at Passchendaele on the Ypres front over Currie's protestations; he correctly estimated the German defences to be very strong. On 26 October 1917 the Canadians and British attacked over deep mud in appalling weather and, as predicted, the operation proved to be a bloodbath. The high ground was finally secured by 10 November; LtGen Currie had predicted that there would be about 16,000 casualties, and the CEF's butcher's bill came to exactly 15,654 killed, missing and wounded. The strategic gains were minimal.

*   *   *

Following the collapse of Russia, which concluded a separate armistice with the Central Powers on 15 December 1917, the German armies on the Western Front were strongly reinforced. Seeking a decisive victory before American troops reached the front in any numbers, the German chief-of-staff Gen Ludendorff launched a massive spring offensive from 21 March 1918. His forces initially achieved spectacular gains, pushing forward some 40 miles (65km) towards Amiens through the front of the British Fifth Army south of Arras, and later further north between La Bassée and Ypres on the Second Army front. In June and July further offensives in the south pushed the French armies back to Château Thierry and Epernay south-west of Reims. However, the tired, ill-supplied German armies became overextended, and were first checked and later counter-attacked successfully by Allied armies including American divisions.

Arras and the 'Hundred Days'

By August 1918 part of the lost ground had been regained, and so had the initiative. General Haig now planned a major surprise attack on the Arras area by the British Third and Fourth Armies reinforced with the Canadian Corps. Well known to the Germans by now as elite assault troops, the corps was shifted to its jumping-off positions in secrecy. General Currie recalled: 'The Canadian Corps was moved down to form the spearhead of that attack. The troops on the right and on the left were ordered to take their time from, and make their advances according to the wishes of, the Canadian Corps.' On 8 August the artillery opened up, more than 400 British tanks lumbered forward, and the infantry advanced; the surprise was complete, and the German line collapsed in what Ludendorff himself later described as the 'black day of the German Army'.

For the first time since 1914 the struggle became a war of movement, and the Canadian Corps proved adept at moving fast in spite of being heavily outnumbered. The 18 divisions of the Third Army and the Canadian Corps faced 33 German divisions, while the Fourth Army's 16 divisions faced another 33. More British divisions were committed, while the French and Americans launched attacks to keep the Germans occupied further south. The Canadian Corps

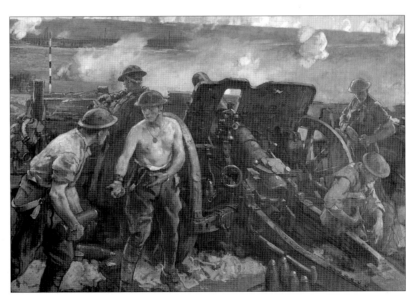

The Vimy Ridge bombardment, 20 March–9 April 1917; a 4.5in howitzer is shown in this detail from a 1919 painting by Richard Jack. Even in the chilling cold and rain the tiring work of serving guns at high rates of fire made men so hot that many worked in shirtsleeves or stripped to the waist. Success at Vimy owed as much to meticulous preparation as to courage in the infantry assault. Many miles of rail tracks, water pipelines and telephone cables were installed, and tunnels were dug that allowed troops to come forward under cover. For two weeks some 983 guns hammered the ridge, and for the first time thorough observation and the reporting of intelligence allowed the Canadians to locate and knock out some 80 per cent of the German batteries before the assault. (Canadian War Museum, Ottawa)

was then tasked by Haig with piercing the Hindenburg Line, which was achieved by 2 September. By mid-October the Germans had lost Cambrai and the BEF was in full pursuit. The Germans made a stand at Valenciennes, but the Canadian Corps attacked and took the positions on 1 November. Thrusting onwards, the Canadians reached Mons by 10 November. Lieutenant Andrews of the 10th CEF Bn wrote:

On November 10 [the officers] were told that hostilities would cease at 11am next day. We still refused to believe it. It was too good to be true. We held a parade at 11am and told the company the war was over. The boys were almost stunned, not a cheer. It was something they had dreamed about but never expected to see. They were going home. It was too soon to worry what was to happen next. The parade dismissed and it gradually dawned on them what it meant.

The 10th CEF marched into Germany as part of the army of occupation on the Rhine. On 13 December, 'the Battalion marched thro the streets of Cologne with fixed bayonets. The people seemed very sullen and many men in the crowd seemed very angry.' It was an omen for 20 years in the future.

* * *

Canadian troops provided garrisons on the Carribean islands of Bermuda and St Lucia; small detachments of engineers operated barges on the Rivers Tigris and Euphrates in Iraq; Canadian instructors went to the United States; a Canadian hospital was set up in Greece to treat Gallipoli casualties; and a sizeable Canadian contingent was sent to Russia.

Intervention in Russia

Following the Russian Revolution, the separate peace concluded by the Bolshevik regime, and the outbreak of civil war between the Red and White armies, in 1918 the Allies decided to secure some of Russia's strategic ports and lines of communication in support of the Whites, whom they attempted to supply and train. In the summer of 1918 contingents from Allied armies occupied Murmansk and Archangel; Canada was requested to provide instructors, and a special mobile unit of 18 officers and 70 NCOs went to join the British in Murmansk during late September. The US contingent at Archangel had no gunners, so on 1 October the 18 officers and 469 men of the 16th Bde, Canadian Field Artillery joined them there, subsequently seeing action against Bolshevik troops.

Meanwhile, Allied forces had also occupied the Pacific port of Vladivostok in Siberia since August 1918. Canada agreed to contribute a force and, from October 1918, the 259th & 260th CEF Bns – numbering some 4,000 men with artillery and other support units – sailed from

Portrait by Sir William Orpen of LtGen Sir Arthur Currie, commander of the CEF from June 1917 to 1919. Rarely in history has a truly outstanding general come from such an unlikely background. An Ontario farm boy, by 1914 Currie was a businessman and militia officer in Vancouver. His talents blossomed in the field, where he had a meteoric rise to senior command. At first glance, Currie had few of the traditional qualities of a dashing military commander; he was physically heavy, with a rather lugubrious expression and a taciturn manner, but he had an outstanding tactical mind. His talents were widely recognized by senior Allied commanders; he was knighted on the battlefield of Vimy by King George V, and succeeded Sir Julian Byng in command of the CEF, which he led to victory and an incomparable reputation. As seen from this painting, Canadian generals wore exactly the same uniform as their British counterparts – though note the fur-collared coat. Currie disliked this portrait, and it was withdrawn from public display in 1923. (Canadian War Museum, Ottawa)

Vancouver to Siberia, joining some 70,000 Japanese and 8,000 American troops around Vladivostok. With the end of the Great War in November, and the apparently inevitable victory of the Bolsheviks over the Whites, the Allied interventions in Russia appeared increasingly futile. Between April and August 1919 the Canadian contingent, which had taken no part in the fighting, was withdrawn from Vladivostok. They were followed by the Allied contingents at Murmansk and Archangel in September and October 1919.

Middle East

Another theatre of war in which small numbers of Canadians served was Palestine and Syria. Following a request for expert bridge-builders, the 1st Cdn Bridging Coy (256 all ranks) was formed from eight of the Canadian Railway Troops battalions then in France. This small unit sailed from Marseilles on 20 September 1918, arriving in Palestine 12 days later. Damascus had fallen on 1 October and it was now vital to extend railway communications to the Syrian capital. To this end the Canadians were ordered to the Yarmuk Valley, arriving on 5 October to work on two of the railway bridges. Heat and fever took a heavy toll: just two weeks later three-quarters of the men were sick and four had died. Nevertheless the work was done, with the help of the Egyptian Labour Corps. The company moved to Hama at the end of October, and worked on restoring the railway until the first week of February 1919. A month later it sailed for England, to rejoin the Railway Troops Depot.

The honours for the most exotic detachment for Canadians probably belong to the party of 15 officers and 26 NCOs 'of strong character' sent to Baghdad, Mesopotamia (now Iraq) in 1918 to join the British 'Dunsterforce' being organized there. Made up of 150 officers and 1,500 men, Dunsterforce had the main purpose of 'organizing, training, and leading native troops to be raised from the tribes of Asia Minor and Mesopotamia', as well as to protect the Baku oilfields in southern Russia – a somewhat ambitious mission statement. The Canadians arrived in Basra in March 1918 and were eventually involved in myriad political and military events in present-day Iraq, Iran and southern Russia, including a coup d'état in Baku. In August a powerful Turkish army attacked the mixed Armenian, White Russian and British force at Baku, which had to be evacuated on 14–15 September 1918; Dunsterforce was disbanded a few days later. The Canadians had provided various cadres for tasks ranging from taking charge of Baku's government treasury to commanding the 24th Armenian Battalion. Most of them returned to their units in Western Europe, but a few chose to serve with irregulars in Armenia; a few joined the newly created North Persian Force, and five

Moving trench stores and supplies up to the front line required such manpower that a battalion in every BEF brigade usually had to be devoted to logistics rather than fighting. In 1916 head straps or 'tump lines', used for load-carrying by Canadian *voyageurs* and woodsmen for centuries, were tried out (apparently first in the 11th Bde, 4th Cdn Div), and soon spread throughout the Corps. This device was so efficient that one 'tump line company' per brigade was found to be enough; this was apparently an element in the CEF's maintenance of four-battalion brigades throughout the war. The tump line was made from oiled leather; web or canvas were 'absolutely useless', as they became 'soggy, stringy and wrinkled' when wet. (*Canadian Defence Quarterly*, October 1928)

23

Men of the Newfoundland Regt in a trench at Suvla Bay, Gallipoli, during autumn 1915. Arriving in Britain in October 1914, the regiment was trained and, in August 1915, sent out to the Mediterranean. Before embarkation they were issued the standard British khaki tropical uniform with the Wolseley helmet, the jacket shoulder straps bearing their brass 'NFLD' title. After a stop in Egypt the Newfoundlanders joined the British 29th Div on the Gallipoli peninsula in September. The regiment suffered its first casualties while manning the trenches there until its evacuation on 16–17 December. (Private collection)

went to the British Military Mission in Siberia. No Canadian casualties were reported, possibly a unique instance in Canada's contributions to the Great War.

The Newfoundland contribution

On 1 July each year Canadians celebrate Canada Day, the national holiday. However, since 1949, when the British colony of Newfoundland became Canada's tenth province, the morning celebrations are initially very solemn, with remembrance ceremonies at the war memorials in St John's and Ottawa: since 1916, 1 July has been a day of mourning in Newfoundland. At about 9.15am on the morning of that day the Newfoundland Regiment 'went over the bags' in front of Beaumont Hamel in the Somme valley; on this first day of the offensive the unit was serving with 88th Bde of the British 29th Div, in VIII Corps of Third Army. At the appointed time, 801 officers and men left their trenches and advanced over the featureless chalky grassland toward the German-fortified village. The attack lasted about an hour; and at roll call the following day, just 68 men of the battalion answered to their names.

Newfoundland's response to Britain's call to arms had been enthusiastic. Nearly 12,000 enlisted in the Newfoundland Regt, the Royal Naval Reserve and the Newfoundland Forestry Corps; this figure represented nearly 10 per cent of the total male population, or more than 35 per cent of young men between the ages of 19 and 35. In October 1914 the Newfoundland Regt's 'First Five Hundred' landed in Britain. In August 1915 the battalion was issued with tropical uniforms, and deployed with the British 29th Div at Suvla Bay, Gallipoli, where it served from October to December. It was then sent with its division to the Western Front and, as related above, was nearly wiped out on the First Day of the Somme. In spite of this disaster the regiment was re-raised, granted the 'Royal' title in recognition of its outstanding sacrifice, and continued to serve on the Western Front until the end of the war, being attached to the 9th (Scottish) Div from September 1918.

Some 1,964 Newfoundlanders joined the Royal Naval Reserve; only seamen and fishermen were eligible. They were scattered throughout the Royal Navy, and 180 lost their lives in the course of the war. The 500-strong Newfoundland Forestry Corps was raised in 1917 and served in Scotland.

UNIFORMS, ARMS & EQUIPMENT

At the beginning of the 20th century Canadian regular and militia units were issued colourful scarlet, dark blue or rifle-green uniforms. Since 1863 the basic kit issued to Canadian volunteers had included a forage

(continued on page 33)

1: Private, 96th Lake Superior Regt, c.1910–14
2: Corporal, 15th Light Horse Regt, c.1908–12
3: Officer, 72nd Seaforth Highlanders of Canada (Vancouver), c.1910–14

1

2

3

A

1: Private at summer camp, undress, 1913–14
2: Officer, Corps of Guides, full dress, c.1910–14
3: Officer, 38th Dufferin Rifles of Canada, 1912–13

B

1: Infantry private, CEF, autumn 1914
2: Infantry private, CEF; England, winter 1914–15
3: Piper, 13th CEF Bn (Royal Highlanders of Canada), 1914–15

C

1: Warrant Officer, 8th CEF Bn, 1915–16
2: Private, 14th CEF Bn, 1915
3: Gunner, Royal Canadian Artillery, 1914–15

D

1: Sniper, Canadian Corps, 1916–18
2: Pte, 43rd CEF Bn (Cameron Highlanders of Canada), 1917–18
3: Pte, 22nd CEF Bn (Canadien-Français), 1917–18

E

1: Officer, 1st Bn Royal Newfoundland Regiment, 1916–18
2: Pte, 31st Coy, Canadian Forestry Corps, 1917–18
3: Sergeant major, Canadian Light Horse, 1916–18

F

1: Lieutenant-colonel, CAMC, 1917
2 & 3: CAMC nursing sisters, 1914–19

1

3

2

BRADFORD WG LIBRARY
100 HOLLAND COURT, BOX 130
BRADFORD, ONT. L3Z 2A7

G

1: Pilot, Royal Flying Corps, 1917–18
2: Seaman, Royal Canadian Navy, 1914–18
3: Lieutenant, RNCVR, 1914–18

H

cap, a tunic or 'frock' and trousers, sometimes with additional items. Individual units also raised funds to improve the basic issue with, usually, full dress items such as helmets or busbies for parades. In cities, the wealthier Volunteer Militia regiments would often raise substantial funds to improve their dress; in rural areas the improvements were usually restricted to a few field officers acquiring full dress uniforms.

The government's traditional policy was to spend as little as possible on defence while keeping up a basic military force. The least expensive way to do this was to keep the tens of thousands of volunteer reservists content with basic 'drill pay' and attractive uniforms. A debate over having cloth dress tunics instead of drill frocks had been settled in 1896, after a fashion, by the issue of serge frocks. These were made more attractive by retaining the arm of service's basic colour, trimmed with facings and piping. Thus, the infantry serge frock was scarlet with dark blue collar, cuffs and shoulder straps, piped at the bottom of the collar, the shoulder straps and the cuffs with white; the latter were finished with a 'crow's foot' trefoil knot, a feature of Canadian infantry uniforms since 1876–77. Gunners had a dark blue frock with scarlet facings and yellow piping; Rifles had rifle-green trimmed with scarlet; cavalry had scarlet or dark blue frocks trimmed with regimental facings depending on their titles as dragoons, hussars, etc. Since the early 1900s basic headdress was a dark blue peaked cap. Regimental badges, worn on the headdress and jacket collar, were increasingly adopted. These uniforms would be issued to last for a period of about five years, so it took years before any major changes in regulations became apparent.

Two Canadian soldiers in August 1917, Vimy Ridge area. This informal picture shows the Canadian pattern khaki shirt with collar, the high-waisted trousers (with khaki suspenders on the left, and belt at the right), and one man (right) wearing high laced field boots. They are posing with medieval-looking German caltrop planks found in trench stores before they could be installed. (Photo in *Panorama de la guerre ...*, 1917)

The debate over khaki

Following the Boer War, khaki clothing became the regulation field dress in the British Army. This development was considered by the authorities in Ottawa and, in April–May 1903, it was approved in principle for Canadian regulars and militiamen. The small regular force thus received a distinct Canadian-pattern khaki clothing issue in addition to the colourful dress and service uniforms. While khaki posed no problems for the small force of regulars, most of the Volunteer Militia had no wish to be deprived of their colourful uniforms. As early as January 1905 the *Canadian Military Gazette* editorialized that 'the Canadian Militia, as a whole [was] thoroughly tired of khaki', and that the government should relent in its issue, 'relegating it to its proper place, the storehouse, in waiting for active service.' The bureaucrats and politicians were reluctant to increase the defence budget to meet the extra cost; and as late as March 1909 the Quartermaster-General was making arrangements for blue, rifle-green and scarlet serge frocks to be issued with peaked 'Naval pattern' caps to the volunteer militiamen. The newly raised Western cavalry regiments

33

also preferred to wear scarlet or dark blue serge jackets, often with Stetson hats, which gave them a dashing look (see Plate A2).

There was, nevertheless, a slow realization that the adoption of khaki was inevitable, and that for rural units in particular it would be the only uniform issue. A few units experimented with making khaki uniforms more attractive by adding facings, but these were doomed to be short-lived (see Plate B3). A landmark decision was made in January 1913 for all volunteers to receive khaki jackets, trousers and peaked caps to last five years; in addition, city units would have colourful cloth tunics, trousers and peaked caps to last nine years. These issues would start once the present clothing had worn out – thus, in 1914, some militia units did not yet have khaki uniforms. With this order came an issue of service clothing – shirts, straw hats, etc. – for use at the summer training camps.

Khaki Canadian pattern uniforms

When, from 1903, khaki uniforms were introduced in Canada, they were inspired by the new British uniforms but adapted to the perceived needs of Canadians. Since they would probably be the only uniforms issued to rural volunteers it was important that they should look smart – smarter than the British jacket, with its loose fit, turndown collar and five large front buttons. The Canadian-pattern khaki jacket had a tighter fit, seven small front buttons and a standing collar; the Canadian trousers were also cut tighter; unlike the collarless 'greyback' British shirt the Canadian pattern was khaki with a turndown collar; and the Canadian khaki peaked cap had a wire reinforcement to keep the crown rigid.

Two privates of the 195th CEF Bn (City of Regina), 1916, provide a good image of the Canadian pattern seven-button khaki jacket issued throughout the war to CEF units raised in Canada. The 195th was organized in Regina, Saskatchewan, from mid-July 1916, but was absorbed into the 32nd Reserve Bn immediately it arrived in Liverpool, England on 11 November 1916. (Library and Archives Canada, C 43258)

To provide some distinction between the various branches of the service, from 1903 the jacket's shoulder straps had a quarter-inch edging of red for infantry, yellow for cavalry, and dark blue with a scarlet central braid for artillery. In August 1914 Sir Sam Hughes decided that units in the CEF would have the entire shoulder straps in facing colours. The branch colours chosen for the troops of the first contingent assembling at Valcartier were blue for infantry, green for rifles, yellow for cavalry, red for artillery and the Corps of Guides, red with yellow central loop for engineers, red with blue loop for ordnance, cherry-red for the medical corps, maroon for the veterinary corps, white with two blue central lines for the service corps, and 'French grey' for signals. Some of these colours changed during the Great War: the medical corps took maroon, while the veterinary corps changed to the cavalry's yellow shoulder strap; the engineers discarded the coloured straps in favour of a small red tab with the letters 'C.E.' in blue worn on the upper sleeve.

From early in the war a yellow metal title 'CANADA' was worn at the outer end of the shoulder straps, although this became official only in 1917. Straps were otherwise usually plain, although there were later additions such as 'CFA' for the field artillery. Collar badges consisted of the letter 'C' for Canada, over the CEF battalion number in the infantry, a grenade or a maple leaf for gunners, and the regimental badge for cavalry, but there were variations throughout the war.

The outbreak of war naturally faced the authorities with a chronic shortage of khaki uniforms. On 10 August 1914, 40,000 uniforms were ordered, followed by another 40,000 in early October made by various Canadian manufacturers, who scrambled to meet the sudden demand. In the following months and years the production figures grew to millions, and a number of variations naturally occurred. Some, but by no means all types encountered are illustrated in this book.

A Royal Canadian Artillery warrant officer (left) with an officer of a CEF Scottish battalion, c.1915. The WO wears an officer's open-collar jacket with shirt and necktie, a fashion assumed by some of this rank early in the war; the photo suggests that this seldom-seen garment was not as well tailored as the officer's jacket. The Canadian military authorities disapproved of this fashion, and by 1916 all WOs were wearing the older officer-style jacket buttoning to the neck (see Plate D1). From his badges, the officer at right probably belongs to the 13th CEF Bn (Royal Highlanders of Canada). (Private collection)

From 1 December 1914 coloured shoulder straps were discontinued and jackets were henceforth supplied with plain khaki straps, but this was not in fact the end of the coloured straps in the CEF (see below). Some jackets were no longer made with pointed cuffs; others assumed a stand-and-fall collar with hooks-and-eyes so they could be worn either standing in Canadian fashion or down in British fashion. Some were seen with five small front buttons but otherwise cut like Canadian jackets.

Once in Europe, the most significant change in the dress of the CEF was the gradual, but never total adoption of the British 1902 khaki service dress jacket. This started in 1915 when replacement uniforms were issued and, together with the adoption of other British items, made many Canadians look very much like their British comrades from 1915–16. There were individual alterations, however. Private Alfred Andrews of the 10th CEF mentioned in January 1916 that 'tunics were issued out but as they were British tunics they didn't have Canadian buttons. We cut the buttons off the old tunics and sewed them on the new ones.' These uniforms were soon worn in action: in February Andrews noted that he and his comrades 'were kicked out of one restaurant because our clothes smelled of the gas we had been thro that day. Our buttons were all discoloured by gas and it took a lot of work getting them cleaned again' (gas turned brass a green colour).

Coloured distinctions

One item that did not quite vanish during 1915 was the coloured shoulder strap. Men of the first Canadian contingent in France insisted on wearing it; this question went up to the highest authorities who, in December 1916, authorized them to be worn only by those men who had 'left Canada in September 1914'. From 1916 the cavalry units were allowed to add multicoloured slip-on ribbons to their shoulder straps, the colours usually being those of the unit's camp flag (see Plate F3). In 1917 another use of coloured shoulder straps was allowed in the 3rd Cdn Div, this time to identify platoon specialists: rifle-grenadiers were assigned blue shoulder straps, Lewis gunners yellow, bombers green and bayonetmen red. Yet another instance was reported in 1917 by Gnr William Kerr: 'it was the privilege of signallers of any unit to wear blue cloth on their shoulder-straps and of this we availed ourselves.'

Soldiers performing certain functions on the Western Front wore a variety of armbands or brassards. For instance, line-of-communications personnel had 'L.ofC.' in black on a red armband; signals had armbands halved blue-above-white; military police had 'MP' in red on black, and stretcher-bearers 'SB' in black on white. Some platoon specialists in the 1st and possibly the 2nd and 4th Cdn Divs used distinguishing armbands instead of shoulder straps: in January 1917, Pte David McLean of the 15th CEF mentioned being 'in the grenade section, that is bombs we use. We wear green bands around our arms.'

Staff officers wore the usual British-style right arm brassards in appropriate colours, sometimes with a maple leaf device: red/white/red for the corps HQ, all red for a divisional HQ and blue for a brigade HQ.

Unit and formation patches

From 1914 Princess Patricia's Canadian Light Infantry wore at the top of each sleeve a red cloth arc with the white title 'P.P.C.L.I.' in addition to the brass national title on the shoulder straps. By September 1916 the need to identify divisions, brigades and units in the BEF at a glance was leading to the unregulated adoption of myriad different 'battle badges' in the form of coloured cloth shapes on the upper sleeves and elsewhere on the khaki jacket. In that month the CEF introduced a unified system of shoulder patches in a variety of shapes and colours. The War Diary of the 24th CEF records that, on 9 September, its 'distinguishing mark of blue rectangle square [sic] surmounted with red semi-circle were sewed on each [jacket's] shoulder of the men' (LAC, RG9, IIID3, 4932). The system for infantry battalions is described in the caption to the illustration on page 44 (and see Plate E2 & E3).

Headgear

The 1905 Canadian-pattern khaki field service cap, with its rigidly stiffened crown, gave a distinct look to CEF men in 1914–15; while this looked smart, it was rather uncomfortable in the trenches and the men often took out the wire stiffener to make the cap more pliable. Headquarters frowned upon this throughout the war although, as early as 1915, many CEF units were also wearing the British-pattern cap with its soft visor and unstiffened crown. Another British headgear popular in the CEF, especially in 1915–16, was the soft 'Gor' Blimey' trench cap with its side flaps attaching over the crown.

In early 1916 the British Mk I steel helmet was gradually issued in the BEF, including the CEF units, and was painted a matt khaki colour. In the Canadian Corps, especially in 1918, some units also painted their unit patches or stencilled the unit badge on helmets; however, many of the surviving examples were probably added after 11 November 1918.

Protective clothing

For winter, Canadians were initially issued with a khaki greatcoat differing from the British pattern in having seven front buttons rather than five. In Canada, where the winter cold is more severe but also much dryer, winter fur caps and sometimes moccasins and snowshoes were issued, but none of these were suitable in Europe. In February 1915 the Canadian Division was also issued with goatskin jackets, fingerless

Pte T.W.Holmes, 4th Canadian Mounted Rifles Regt, photographed in January 1918. Note the crimson ribbon for the Victoria Cross, which this 19-year-old soldier earned for outstanding heroism at Passchendaele on 26 October 1917; since January 1916 his regiment had been absorbed into the CMR battalions of 8th Bde, serving as infantry in the 3rd Division. The stand-and-fall collar of the Canadian-pattern seven-button jacket is made nearly 'standing' by two hooks-and-eyes, and note the rifle pads on both shoulders – features often seen in photos of Canadian Corps soldiers. The 3rd CMR Bn battle badges can just be seen on his upper sleeve: the triangle of the third battalion of a brigade, in the red of the second brigade of a division, here worn above the 'French grey' (light blue-grey) rectangle of 3rd Cdn Div – initially the latter had been black, but was changed for better visibility. The 4th CMR Regt had a distinctive moose-head badge, retained here on the cap and collars. (Library and Archives Canada, PA 2352) woollen mitts and mufflers. As the war went on, British greatcoats became very common, as did the brown leather sleeveless jerkin, and khaki wool Balaclava helmet. Canadian boots also proved unsuitable for conditions in Europe and British replacements were issued from the end of January 1915. In the muddy trenches a variety of waterproofed or rubber boots were worn by Canadian troops; one popular type was the 'Larrigan' boot, reaching high up the calf and lacing in front. Another popular item mentioned by Pte David McLean of the 15th CEF in November 1916 was 'hip rubber boots when in the trenches so we can keep fairly dry' – i.e. trench waders, as often issued in the British Army.

Highland uniforms

The dress of Canadian Highlanders generally followed that of British Highlanders, with kilt, sporran, hose, and the Glengarry and/or the Balmoral (tam-o'shanter) as headdress; all of these items were distinctive to each Highland CEF battalion (see Table 2). In 1914 the khaki jacket was usually of the cut-away doublet style as worn by British Highlanders; while this remained the usual dress throughout the war the higher-numbered CEF battalions might also be seen wearing the general issue Canadian or British jackets. Again like British Highlanders, the khaki kilt apron, with the integral pocket which took the place of the sporran, was also issued for wear in the trenches or for fatigue duties. Early in the war the supply of tartan cloth for kilts became a problem. Some of the setts initially chosen for CEF battalions did not exist in the British Army's supply system and were quickly changed. A simplified 'khaki tartan' was also devised and came into wear in some units during 1915; this had a khaki ground with a simple windowpane chequering of vertical and horizontal stripes made up of narrow red/green/dark blue lines. By April 1917, khaki (or 'drab') kilts were issued to all Highlanders in reserve units in England, these being exchanged for tartan by men who were sent to a front line Highland unit as reinforcements. By then the distinct Highland dress was seen as both costly and troublesome, and the supply services demanded that all CEF Highlanders be issued trousers. Apparently these were anyway often worn instead of kilts in the trenches; Pte McLean of the 15th CEF mentioned in December 1916 that 'we have the pants just now but there is always some of the officers wearing the kilt'. The bureaucrats eventually got their way, and by November 1917 only trousers were issued to reinforcement drafts. A year later kilts were no longer issued, but nearly all Canadian Highlanders still possessed a kilt to wear when the Armistice came.

Lt A.H.Finlay, 16th CEF Bn (Canadian Scottish), c.1915, wearing his battalion's dress uniform. Note the dark blue Glengarry with a band of red and white dicing; the 'doublet' cut of the jacket, including the cuffs with their distinctive arrangement of the officer's cuff ranking; and the Mackenzie tartan breeches worn by officers of this unit. (Library and Archives Canada, PA 7187)

Painting by Eric Kennington showing a squad of the 16th CEF Bn (Canadian Scottish) in November 1918. The men are shown without helmets or kilt aprons; they wear khaki Balmorals, cut-away jackets, Mackenzie tartan kilts, red garter flashes on their hose, and have web equipment and SMLE rifles and bayonets. The soldiers shown are actually portraits of surviving and fallen members of the unit. The ranks of Canadian Scottish units were not exclusively filled with Scots; many French-Canadians are recorded wearing the kilt and, at the centre of this painting, we see an African-Canadian. Note that he lacks shoulder titles, apparently wears pistol equipment, and carries a small rolled flag instead of a rifle. (Canadian War Museum, Ottawa)

Rank distinctions

Most NCOs wore the same uniform and equipment as junior ranks, with the appropriate rank chevrons on both upper sleeves. Warrant officers had a jacket of the same cut as the commissioned officer's jacket worn between 1904 and 1912, buttoning to the throat. They also wore brown leather Sam Browne belts like commissioned officers rather than the soldier's webbing equipment. Rank badges for Canadian NCOs and warrant officers were the same as in the British Army.

Officers followed British dress regulations quite closely. The open jacket collar exposing a light khaki shirt and tie was approved for Canadian officers in February 1913. The major difference between Canadian and British officers at the beginning of the war lay in the placement of rank badges; many Canadian officers initially did not have the woven cuff ranking system displayed by British officers, and wore only gilt metal rank badges on the shoulder straps, as required by Canadian regulations. Once overseas this was amended; ranks began to be displayed on the cuffs; photos show that some officers took their time to adopt this, while others wore both metal shoulder strap and woven cuff badges. Orders of September 1916 confirmed that the rank badges were to be worn on the cuffs. Photos show officers with additional badges on their divisional sleeve patches, e.g. a gold 'II' within 'C' in 2nd Cdn Div, and a gold maple leaf in 4th Division. It should be mentioned that officers quite often wore privates' jackets and equipment in the trenches to avoid the attention of German snipers.

Personal equipments

From 1901, Canadian troops used the M1899 Canadian-pattern Oliver equipment, a fairly complicated set of accoutrements made of dark brown leather; it could be configured in various ways, but its most distinctive feature was a large ventral pouch. Meanwhile Britain was adopting the 08 web equipment and, in 1913, Canada ordered and received 5,000 trial sets of this. Except for five battalions, the troops in the Canadian Division went over to England with Oliver equipment. The British were not impressed with this, and the Canadian Division received web equipment before proceeding to France in early 1915. Proponents of the Canadian leather accoutrements reacted by making improvements that resulted in the M1915 Oliver set, which was enthusiastically endorsed by Sir Sam Hughes. This pattern had two pouches holding 100 rounds each, and various other features such as a frog for the entrenching tool. The 2nd Cdn Div left Canada equipped with the M1915 Oliver set, but this was also replaced with 08 webbing before they went into the trenches in September 1915.

Sir Sam Hughes did not give up, and a third variant of the Oliver 'dismounted equipment pattern' was issued in early 1916 to all CEF units in Canada and to the 4th Cdn Div when it left England for France that August. This version had a new canvas haversack, and two leather pouches of 75 rounds capacity; the fastening strap arrangement made these look as if they were upside down (see Plate F2). The 4th Div did not wear this 1916 Oliver equipment for long, and it was replaced in early October 1916 with British 08 webbing by direct order of Gen Haig. Other units followed suit: on 26 November 1916, shortly before the battalion was broken up for reinforcements, Pte Samuel G.Barter of the 140th CEF in England noted that 'we turned in our leather Oliver equipment and got Web equipment today'. When Barter and his comrades joined the 26th Bn in France, all had web equipment. However, some units behind the lines in France appear to have continued using Oliver equipment, as did units in Canada.

Rifles: the Ross and the Short Magazine Lee Enfield

Canadian soldiers arriving in Europe in 1914–1915 were armed with the .303in Ross rifle manufactured in Canada, to a design by Sir Charles Ross, 9th Baronet of Balnagown (1872–1942), for a rifle initially meant for hunting and target-shooting. During the Boer War the Canadian government sought to re-arm the Volunteer Militia; unable to convince a British manufacturer to make Lee Enfield rifles in Canada, the government accepted a suggestion by Sir Charles to try a military version of his rifle. Successful trials were held, and in 1902 an initial order was placed for the North West Mounted Police and the Marine Department with the Ross Rifle Company's new factory in Québec City. In 1905 the Volunteer Militia started receiving the Ross. Although there were initial problems in design and production, adjustments were made; the Mk III Ross rifle introduced in 1910 won an enviable reputation at international target matches such as those held at Bisley in England. From 1912 all units of the Canadian regular troops and Volunteer Militia were equipped with the Ross Mk III.

The Ross Mk III featured a slightly convex butt stock and lower profile; barrel length was 30.5in (77.5cm), and overall length 50.25in (128.3cm). It had an extended 5-round box magazine forward of the trigger guard, and took standard British rimmed .303in ammunition; the Mk III could be loaded from stripper clips. The 'straight-pull' bolt had internal turning locking lugs; the barrel had four-groove rifling with a left-hand twist and one turn every 10in (25.4cm); there was an adjustable rear sight mounted on the receiver bridge, and a blade front sight. No carbine version of this rifle was made; CEF gunners and cavalrymen were armed with Lee Enfields before going to France.

Following the declaration of war, the Canadian government immediately ordered tens of thousands of Ross Mk III rifles, and in the next two years some 400,000 were produced of which nearly 130,000 went overseas with the CEF. However, although an accurate weapon,

A major of the *22e bataillon canadien-français*, the famous '*Vingt-deux*' or 'Van-doos', photographed on 21 June 1918 at Bellecourt; he sports a pinned cravat rather than a collar and tie, and wears the ribbon of the Military Cross. His cap bears the 22nd's bi-metal badge: a silver crowned garter, coat-of-arms and '22' set on a gilt beaver and log with the motto '*Je Me Souviens*'. On his shoulder straps are the crown of his rank above the national title, and on his lapels 'C' above '22'. The sleeve patches (see commentary to Plate E3) are a red disc above the dark blue rectangle of 2nd Cdn Div, with the officer's addition of a gold 'II' set within a 'C'. (IWM CO 2774) once in the trenches the Ross revealed itself to be unequal to extended use under the conditions of the modern battlefield. The bolt tended to bear on one of the locking lugs, burring its edge, and the rifle was subject to malfunctions when mud and dirt got into the action. Men reported their rifles jamming during rapid fire – there were cases of soldiers in battle having to kick the bolt to force it open. It also suffered from weak extraction, and might even chamber and fire a round with the bolt lugs unlocked (with potentially fatal consequences); indeed, there were general problems with its handling of British-made as opposed to Canadian-made ammunition. Stories of Canadian soldiers in action scrambling to grab the SMLEs from dead British soldiers spread like wildfire, and more than 3,000 Canadians were documented as having done so at Second Ypres. The Canadian Division was re-armed with the SMLE in June 1915. When all this bad news got back to Canada the media and parliamentary opposition confronted a stubborn Sir Sam Hughes, and eventually the worst Canadian political scandal of the war forced Prime Minister Sir Robert Borden to relent. Meanwhile, Gen Sir Douglas Haig, C-in-C of the British Expeditionary Force, simply gave orders for a change of rifles. By August 1916 the 2nd and 3rd Cdn Divs in France were being re-equipped with the SMLE Mk I and Mk III; the 4th Cdn Div was re-armed on its arrival in France in September, and some SMLEs were also provided for the 5th Div in England.

A sergeant of a Canadian Scottish unit armed with a Ross rifle to demonstrate the use of the 'MacAdams trench shield shovel'. This novel device had a hole large enough to admit a rifle, and in theory was supposed to protect the soldier. The enthusiastic Sir Sam Hughes rushed one of his secretaries, Miss Ena MacAdams, to the Patent Office to sign the official documents; she thus gave her name to the 25,000 shovels bought in Philadelphia at the rather high cost of $1.35 each. Issued to the 2nd Cdn Div in 1915, they turned out to be useless, and were never used except when worn slung at inspections. These shovels soon caused a political scandal; they were recalled into Ordnance stores and sold as scrap metal for $1,400, being replaced with the British entrenching tool. In fairness to Sir Sam and his acolytes, several Great War armies tried out various devices for personal protection which had no more merit than the notorious MacAdams shovel. (Private collection)

However, this was not quite the end of the Ross rifle. Still one of the finest target rifles in the world, it continued to be used on the Western Front by Canadian snipers, who could give expert care to their individual weapons and did not need a rapid-fire capability. Others were used for training (including 20,000 sold to the US for that purpose in 1917), and issued to reserve troops. Troops in Canada also continued to use the Ross; and eventually another 67,090 went to the British Home Guard in World War II.

Nevertheless, from August 1916 onwards the overwhelming majority of Canadian troops overseas carried the British SMLE, normally the Mk III. Introduced in 1907, this very robust and reliable .303in weapon had a detachable ten-round magazine, and a safety-design bolt handle that turned through about 60 degrees to lock down on the right side. Small arms ammunition was produced in Canada at the Québec arsenal from 1885, and between 1916 and 1922 another arsenal operated in Lindsay, Ontario, to meet the increased demand.

Ordnance

In the early part of the war the demand for military equipment and supplies of all sorts increased overwhelmingly, but on the whole the procurement and supply system – mainly the Canadian Ordnance Corps and the Canadian Army Service Corps – met the demand. Depots were set up in Canada and in England; and when Canadian Corps troops could not obtain supplies of arms, uniforms or equipment from Canadian sources they could call upon British stores. Eventually, in 1917, part of the responsibility for supplying the Canadians was turned over to the British; from then on, it did not matter so much if items were Canadian or British so long as they got to the men swiftly.

Before the war Canadian artillery had re-armed with the new British 18-pdr guns, which became the mainstay of the CEF field artillery; the older 12-pdr guns were the main artillery training weapon in Canada. During the Great War, Canadian ordnance went from a few dozen modern field guns (first fired at the enemy on 2 March 1915), to thousands of guns of all sorts. By the later part of the war each Canadian field brigade had three 18-pdr batteries and one 4.5in howitzer battery. The heavy siege batteries on the Western Front were largely armed with the British 6in howitzer and even heavier pieces. The expenditure of ammunition could be very high: at Vimy Ridge, nearly 12,000 rounds were fired on Easter Monday of 1917. The Canadian Railway Troops installed and operated narrow-gauge railways leading right up to the batteries to keep up the supply of ammunition.

Another aspect of Canadian logistics was the nation's tremendous effort in supplying ammunition to all the British forces. In 1914 Canada had agreed to supply up to 4,000 shells a week, but geared up to provide much more. By 1917 Canadian factories supplied half of the shells used by the British forces; by the end of the war they had supplied 25 million shrapnel shells, 41 million other complete projectiles, 48 million shell cases and 148 million pounds of explosives.

An original armoured car of the Canadian Motor Machine Gun Bde, c.1918. This unit – originally the 1st Automobile MG Bde, raised in 1914 – was the brainchild of Maj Raymond Brutinel, an emigrant from France who had become a Canadian millionaire. It initially had nine officers and 114 men, to man eight armoured cars (paid for by a group of patriotic citizens), armed with two Colt 'potato-digger' machine guns; this was the first motorized MG unit raised in the British Empire. The unit eventually had 20 of these MG carriers, built by Autocar of Ardmore, PA, USA; they served in France until 1918. The vehicle shown here, armed with the later Vickers MGs, had a 2-ton chassis, with 5mm front and 3mm rear armour; powered by a 22hp engine, it could reach a maximum of 25mph (40km/h) on roads. On the front of the olive-green hull note the brigade marking (top left), above a dark red arrow (the usual MG symbol) and a bright red bar on a white panel, together with a tactical sign and vehicle letter in white. The arrow and bar were also painted on the front of the men's steel helmets. (Canadian War Museum, Ottawa)

SELECT BIBLIOGRAPHY

The History and Heritage Directorate at the Canadian Forces HQ holds a vast number of records pertaining to the Great War and many files on units, organization and logistics have been consulted for this study. The Canadian Letters and Images Project, a co-operative endeavour by Malaspina University College and University of Western Ontario, has put for consultation on-line an impressive number of diaries, letters and photos in private collections of the Great War. Library and Archives Canada (uniting the former National Library and National Archives of Canada) has extensive records pertaining to the Great War including the unit War Diaries, many of which are accessible on-line. The author was kindly permitted to consult the extensive diaries and notes of Samuel G. Barter in the possession of his descendant.

Chappell, Mike, *The Canadian Army at War* (Osprey, MAA 164, 1985) A much recommended companion to this study, covering representative troops from the Boer War to the Korean War.

Chappell, Mike, *British Infantry Equipments 1908–2000* (Osprey, MAA 182, 2000)

Currie, Arthur, 'The last hundred days of the war', *The Empire Club of Canada Speeches 1919* (Toronto, The Empire Club of Canada, 1920)

Duguid, A.F., *A Question of Confidence: the Ross Rifle in the Trenches* (Ottawa, Service Publications, 1999)

Duguid, A.F., *Official History of the Canadian Forces in the Great War, Vol.1* (Ottawa, 1938)

Gagnon, Jean-Pierre, *Le 22e bataillion (canadien-français) 1914–1919* (Ottawa & Québec, Dept of National Defence & Université Laval, 1986) The fundamental and outstanding socio-military study on French Canada in the war as well as a unit history.

Graves, Donald E., *Century of Service: the History of the South Alberta Light Horse* (Toronto, Robin Brass Studio, 2005) A fine, well-illustrated study that covers early western light horse units.

Greenhous, Brereton, & Stephen J.Harris, *Canada and the Battle of Vimy Ridge, 9–12 April 1917* (Ottawa, Supply & Services Canada, 1992)

Law, Clive M., *Khaki: Uniforms of the Canadian Expeditionary Force* (Ottawa, Service Publications, 1997). A fine source on this topic; unique data on various types of badges and signs.

Legault, Roch, & Jean Lamarre, ed., *La Première Guerre mondiale et le Canada* (Montréal, Méridien, 1999)

Lucy, Roger V., *Tin Lids: Canadian Combat Helmets* (Ottawa, Service Publications, 1997) The outstanding source.

Nicholson, G.W.L., *The Canadian Expeditionary Force 1914–1919* (Ottawa, 1962)

Ranie, William F., ed, *To the Thunderer His Arms: The Royal Canadian Ordnance Corps* (Lincoln, Ontario, 1984)

Report of the Ministry: Overseas Military Forces of Canada 1918 (London, 1919)

'Your motherland will never forget'; in fact, homecoming veterans were left to cope on their own with little help from the government. The nation had been deeply traumatized by the losses of the Great War, and wanted to forget, heal its wounds and march into a promising future. Hundreds of thousands of ex-soldiers had to undertake a new struggle for social justice; they organized the Canadian Legion – still one of the largest associations in Canada – and obtained some redress from the politicians in the 1920s. This plate by Joseph Simpson, published in *Canada in Khaki* during 1919, shows the usual appearance of the CEF soldier by the end of the war. The souvenir German *Pickelhaube* helmets are not artistic embellishment; it seems that tens of thousands of these came back to Canada with the returning troops.

Stewart, Charles H., *'Overseas'; The Lineages and Insignia of the Canadian Expeditonary Force 1914–1919* (Toronto, 1971)

Summers, Jack L., *Tangled Web: Canadian Infantry Accoutrements 1855–1985* (Bloomfield, Museum Restoration Service, 1985) An outstanding source on both Canadian and British equipments.

Tucker, Gilbert Norman, *The Naval Service of Canada: Its Official History, Vol.1* (Ottawa, 1952)

Tyler, Grant, *Drab Serge and Khaki Drill* (Parks Canada, Western Canada Service Centre internal manual, 2003) Superlative study of Canadian combat jackets from 1899.

Wise, S.F., *Canadian Airmen and the First World War: The Official History of the Royal Canadian Air Force, Vol.1* (Ottawa & Toronto, 1980)

THE PLATES

A1: Private, 96th Lake Superior Regiment, c.1910–14

This figure shows the typical uniform worn by many Canadian Volunteer Militia infantrymen from 1896 right up to the time of the Great War, especially in rural units. This militiaman wears the M1896 Canadian serge frock with breast pockets, which was similar for nearly all infantry units – scarlet with brass buttons; dark blue collar, cuffs and shoulder straps edged with white, the cuff piping finished with a 'crow's foot'. It was worn with dark blue trousers with a narrow scarlet stripe, and a stiff peaked (visored) cap with scarlet piping. The brown leather equipment is the basic belt order of the M1899 Oliver set; the standard infantry weapon from 1905 was the Canadian-made Ross rifle.

A2: Corporal, 15th Light Horse Regiment, c.1908–12

The new regiments of Volunteer Militia cavalry raised in Western Canada at the beginning of the 20th century usually assumed a somewhat 'frontier' style, featuring the popular Stetson hat with a 'Montana peak' made famous by the North West Mounted Police and by Canadian mounted rifles in South Africa. The 15th Light Horse was formed in Calgary, Alberta, in 1905. Its uniform consisted of a scarlet serge frock with yellow collar and cuffs, dark blue trousers with double yellow stripes, Stetson hats, brown cavalry accoutrements and laced boots. It was armed with the M1894 .303in Lee-Metford Mk I carbine (40in long and with a six-round detachable magazine), until issued Ross rifles in about 1912. It also had a squad armed with lances for parades, as well as a band. This figure is based on photos of the unit in 1908–12. (After Donald E.Graves, *Century of Service ... –* see Bibliography)

A3: Officer, 72nd Seaforth Highlanders of Canada (Vancouver), c.1910–14

Several Canadian volunteer regiments, especially those raised in cities, were uniformed as Highland regiments. They often took the name and, except for the badge, wore the uniform of a famous Highland regiment of the British Army. In July 1910 approval was given to form the 72nd Regt in Vancouver, prescribing that its uniform 'would be the same as the Seaforths of the Imperial Service, with the Mackenzie tartan.' Thus officers of the 72nd wore scarlet doublets with buff facings, gold buttons and lace, a feather bonnet with white hackle, Mackenzie tartan plaid, sporran with six gold tassels, and red-and-white hose. In spite of the expense, most officers of regiments in Canadian cities purchased full dress uniforms, those of Highlanders and hussars being the most expensive. (After B.McEvoy & A.H. Finlay, *History of the 72nd Canadian Infantry Battalion, Seaforth Highlanders of Canada*, Vancouver, 1920)

A Canadian-pattern seven-button khaki jacket, c.1917–18, with the British turndown collar (featuring two hooks-and-eyes to make it stand) and rifle pads on both shoulders – an example of the improvements made to this pattern during the war. While most of the CEF eventually had the British five-button jacket, modified Canadian-pattern jackets were also seen. (Grenville Museum, Québec)

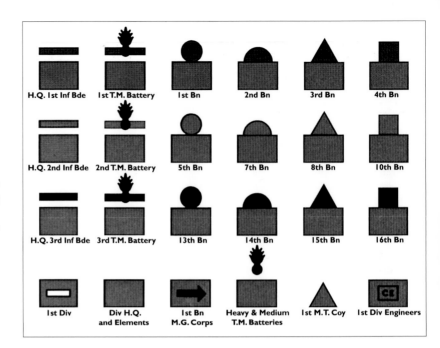

Distinguishing upper sleeve patches of the 1st Cdn Div, 1916–19, as worn from September 1916. The basic rectangle identified the division: 1st, red; 2nd, dark blue; 3rd, light blue-grey ('French grey'); 4th, medium green. The shape above the rectangle identified the battalions within each infantry brigade: disc, half-circle, triangle and square for first to fourth in seniority. The colours of these battalion patches identified the brigade within the division: medium green, red and dark blue for the first to third. Dark blue grenades and bars in brigade colours identified trench mortar and dark red arrows machine gun units; there were also many other types for artillery, cavalry and other corps troops. (Dept of National Defence, 71-844)

B1: Private at summer camp, undress, 1913–14

From 1913 all units were to be issued khaki jackets, trousers and caps, with 'service clothing as required for camp'. The latter included khaki shirts of the Canadian model, with turndown collar, four buttons and a left breast pocket; and summer straw hats with wide brims turned up on the left side. The khaki trousers were held up by off-white suspenders (braces). The Oliver pattern belt with 'snake' clasp, bayonet frog and scabbard for the Ross rifle bayonet was only worn 'under arms', i.e. when the rifle was carried. By 1914 many units had been issued this undress kit, which was also worn by the CEF volunteers at Camp Valcartier. The straw hats were left behind but other items were taken to England in autumn 1914. (Minutes of the Militia Council, 1913)

B2: Officer, Corps of Guides, full dress, c.1910–14

This corps was an intelligence staff unit organized in 1903, primarily made up of volunteer officers assisted by a small company of 27 mounted NCOs and men in each military district. It was the very first Canadian unit to adopt a khaki uniform for its full dress. This consisted of a lancer-style jacket with scarlet facings, khaki lace, cap lines and shoulder cords, khaki girdle with two scarlet stripes, khaki trousers with a scarlet stripe 1½in (3.8cm) wide, and a white helmet with a khaki and scarlet puggaree. The corps was disbanded in 1929.

B3: Officer, 38th Dufferin Rifles of Canada, 1912–13

With the inevitable advent of khaki uniforms, Volunteer Militia officers sought ways to make the new and rather drab clothing more attractive – this was crucial to attract recruits. In about 1911–12 some Rifle regiment officers thought of changing the collar, cuffs and shoulder straps on the standard khaki issue jacket, and the band of the cap, to rifle-green edged with scarlet. The attractive result was worn by some officers of the 2nd and 38th Rifle Regts; the latter unit even received permission, in March 1912, for the whole regiment to wear 'coloured collar and cuffs' on its khaki jackets, but it is uncertain if this actually went into effect. In

any event, it was short-lived: in February 1913 the new British officer's jacket with open collar, shirt and tie was ordered for Canadian officers. (Minutes of the Militia Council, 1912–13)

C1: Infantry private, Canadian Expeditionary Force, autumn 1914

This figure shows the typical fully equipped Canadian infantry soldier as he left Canada and arrived in England. He wears the Canadian field cap with its rigid crown; the Canadian khaki jacket with standing collar and seven front buttons; more tightly tailored trousers than the British model, with puttees and shoes. Most Canadian troops had the brown leather M1899 Oliver equipment, and all carried the Ross Mk III rifle. CEF battalion badges varied greatly, but many had the shape of Canada's maple leaf. The dark blue shoulder straps on the infantry jacket brought some colour to an otherwise drab outfit, and proved very popular in the CEF.

C2: Infantry private, CEF, winter dress; England, 1914–15

At a distance the Canadian-made greatcoat looked much the same as the British pattern, but it had seven brass buttons down the front rather than five. The fall collar was also wider, and had a hook-and-eye arrangement to make the top half 'stand' — although this feature seems not to have been widely used. This coat was initially the standard issue for the CEF, but as time went on the British pattern became prevalent among Canadian soldiers on the Western Front.

C3: Piper, 13th CEF Battalion (Royal Highlanders of Canada), 1914–15

This unit was mainly made up of officers and men from Montréal's 5th Royal Highland Regt, the senior Highland unit in Canada. Its men wore the British pattern khaki Highland cut-away 'doublet' jacket with five buttons and a fall collar, here apparently smartened up at unit level. The battalion's tartan was the Black Watch sett except for the pipe band, which had Royal Stewart kilts and pipe bags; the pipe

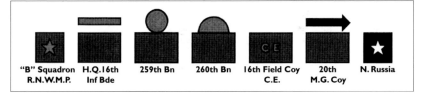

"B" Squadron R.N.W.M.P. | H.Q.16th Inf Bde | 259th Bn | 260th Bn | 16th Field Coy C.E. | 20th M.G. Coy | N. Russia

Distinguishing patches worn on the upper sleeves by the Canadian units sent to Siberia and North Russia in 1919. In Siberia the formation rectangle was pale violet, the unit symbols a red bar, disc, semicircle, letters 'CE' and a dark red arrow. (Left) The RNWMP detachment sent to help fight the Bolsheviks wore – ironically – a red star on a violet square; the North Russia detachment sign (right) was a dark blue square with a white star. (Dept of National Defence, 71-844)

ribbons tied to the drones were a mix of Black Watch and Royal Stewart tartans. The dress sporran was white with two black tails. Pipers also had black-and-red hose with red garters and, early in the war, their headdress was a dark blue Glengarry with a red tourri but no dicing. Indeed, apart from badges, the dress of the 13th CEF was the service uniform of the 5th Regiment. Its pipers made an impressive arrival at St.Nazaire, France, in February 1915 with the Canadian Division, an event commemorated by a large canvas by Edgar Bundy that now hangs in Canada's Senate chamber.

D1: Warrant Officer, 8th CEF Battalion, 1915–16
This figure is based on photos of a warrant officer of this Rifle unit from Winnipeg, which was nicknamed the 'Little Black Devils'. The 8th CEF was the only official Rifle unit in the 1st Cdn Div, and had rifle-green shoulder straps rather than blue as in other infantry battalions. Warrant officers wore a uniform midway between that of commissioned officers and enlisted men. The most notable item was the M1904 officer's khaki jacket, which had a closed collar until the open collar with shirt and tie was introduced for commissioned rank; warrant officers continued to wear the officer's earlier style, but with their own rank badges. Warrant officers had brown leather Sam Browne belts and officer-style breeches, but also wore enlisted men's puttees and boots.

D2: Private, 14th CEF Battalion, 1915
Of the changes made to the equipment and uniforms of the CEF battalions as they were deployed on the Western Front from early 1915, the most visible was the replacement of the leather Oliver equipment with the British 08 web equipment. Many Canadians, like this soldier, also obtained the soft British field service cap in preference to the stiffened Canadian type. Brass 'CANADA' shoulder strap titles became widespread, as did collar badges with 'C' for Canada above the battalion number. The blue shoulder straps were seen on the jackets of nearly all Canadian infantrymen until the summer of 1915. Thereafter, uniform replacements with plain straps appeared, and re-inforcements arrived wearing various patterns of Canadian or British jackets, but the blue straps would be granted as a continuing distinction of the first contingent to arrive. The standard weapon at this date remained the Ross Mk III.

D3: Gunner, Royal Canadian Artillery, 1914–15
The field batteries that went to Europe in 1914 and 1915 wore the Canadian seven-button khaki jacket with (initially) red branch-of-service shoulder straps, the stiff Canadian cap, breeches, puttees, boots and spurs. Later on heavy artillerymen wore trousers and discontinued the spurs. The equipment consisted of the M1903 British 50-round bandolier to carry their rifle ammunition. The red shoulder straps seem to have vanished gradually during 1915, and the British five-button jacket was widely issued, but Canadian jackets were still occasionally seen as late as 1918. Although steel helmets were issued during 1916, photos of the period show gunners serving guns still wearing peaked caps, jackets and – sometimes – bandoliers. The RCA gunners had a brass cap badge nearly identical to that of their Royal Artillery comrades except that the motto 'UBIQUE' above the gun motif was replaced with 'CANADA'. The brass collar badges were the general issue Canadian maple leaf type.

E1: Sniper, Canadian Corps, 1916–18
Some of the most lethal soldiers in the Canadian Corps were snipers; most of them had been raised in the backwoods and had handled rifles since they were children, and many of them were Canadian Indians. Henry Norwest, son of a Cree and French Métis couple from Alberta, joined the 50th CEF Bn in 1915; he achieved a sniping record of 115 kills. Francis Pegahmagabow, an Ojibwa from the Parry Island Band in Ontario who joined the 1st CEF Bn in 1914, was another outstanding sniper and trench raider, who became the most decorated aboriginal in Canada, with awards including the Military Medal with two bars; he survived the war, and went on to become chief of his band. Snipers wore the standard uniform without any badges or coloured patches; a common head covering shown here was the khaki 'sniper's hood'. The usual weapon was the Ross rifle mounted with a telescopic sight, here the American 5.2x power Warner & Swasey. (Law, Clive M., *Without Warning: Canadian Sniper Equipment in the 20th Century*, Ottawa, Service Publications, 2004.)

E2: Private, 43rd CEF Battalion (Cameron Highlanders of Canada), 1917–18
This figure is typical of the fully equipped Canadian Highlander of Vimy Ridge or Passchendaele. He wears the steel helmet with a linen cover, and a British-supplied Highland cut-away jacket with his regimental collar badges. From September 1916 a unified system of battle insignia – cloth patches worn at both shoulders to identify units, brigades and divisions at a glance – was introduced in the CEF; that for the 43rd was a disc (for senior battalion) in dark blue (for third brigade, in this case 9th Bde), over the light blue or 'French grey' rectangle of the 3rd Canadian Division. The kilt – of Cameron of Erracht tartan for the 43rd – is covered with the khaki apron in front; he wears khaki hose and puttees, and black boots. His 08 web equipment, small box respirator slung on the chest and SMLE Mk III rifle are standard British issue.

E3: Private, 22nd CEF Battalion (Canadien-Français), 1917–18
This soldier serves in the only completely French-Canadian CEF battalion maintained on the Western Front, all others having been dispersed into mainly Anglophone units. He wears the usual dress in the trenches during the colder

seasons. The head was kept warm by a khaki wool 'balaclava', and the sleeveless goatskin jacket was a popular item for wear over the khaki jacket. Photos of the 22nd show the men wearing both Canadian- and British-pattern jackets. They might also wear rubber boots or these 'trench waders' in particularly wet conditions. The cloth unit and formation signs adopted for the *Vingt-Deux* on 10 September 1916 were a red disc (senior battalion, second brigade – here, 5th Bde) over the dark blue rectangle of 2nd Canadian Division. The steel helmet had been issued since early in 1916, and these battle insignia were later painted on some helmets in the 22nd Bn – a fairly widespread practice in the Canadian Corps during 1918. The 22nd was armed with the SMLE Mk III from August 1916. (Joseph Chaballe, *Histoire du 22e Bataillon canadien-français 1914–1919*, Montréal, Chanteclair, 1952; Vénat, Pierre, *Les 'Poilus' québécois de 1914–1918*, Montréal, Méridien, 1999–2000, 2 vols.; regimental museum of the Royal 22e Régiment, La Citadelle, Québec)

F1: Officer, 1st Battalion Royal Newfoundland Regiment, 1916–18

Although part of Canada only since 1949, Newfoundland is closely linked to the colonial history of Canada. In 1914 many Newfoundlanders volunteered and the Newfoundland Regiment was formed, nicknamed 'the blue puttees' from the colour of their legwear in the first months of the war. Once in Europe the battalion was issued standard British Army khaki uniforms, equipment and armament, with the brass title 'NFLD' at the end of the jacket shoulder straps. The

regimental badge, worn here on the SD cap and the collars, was a moose head, the traditional insignia of Newfoundland, above a scroll. This figure is based on photos of regimental officers; his uniform conforms to the pattern worn by officers in the BEF, but he retains the metal shoulder strap ranking worn by all Canadian officers in 1914. When divisional insignia were worn, that of the 'incomparable 29th' was a broad, shallow scarlet triangle on the upper sleeves. The Newfoundland battalion, rebuilt after its virtual annihilation on the First Day of the Somme in 1916, went on to serve for the last two months of the war in 9th Div, which wore a white metal thistle badge pinned through a blue disc on the upper sleeves. (G.W.L.Nicholson, *The Fighting Newfoundlander*, Government of Newfoundland, 1964)

F2: Private, 31st Company, Canadian Forestry Corps, 1917–18

This figure is based on a photo of Pte R.Tilburt, a native of Chicago who came to Canada as a boy in 1907. Ten years later he joined the Canadian Forestry Corps at Sussex, New Brunswick, and was sent to France. The Canadian pattern khaki tunic is worn with the rigid peaked cap, but the most noticeable feature is his Canadian M1916 Oliver 'dismounted equipment'. This featured two cartridge pouches with two small straps buckling on the top, giving them an odd, 'upside-down' look. Most of the Canadian Corps continued to wear web equipment, but the M1916 Oliver set was issued to some units, including the Canadian Forestry Corps. For their forestry work, the men usually wore a soft hat with a brim, a khaki shirt and work trousers. (Canadian Letters and Images Project, Malaspina University College and University of Western Ontario)

F3: Sergeant major, Canadian Light Horse, 1916–18

Photos taken in France show that these troopers from the Western provinces retained their distinctive Stetson hats when not in the front lines. Many NCOs and men pinned the badge of their Volunteer Militia regiment to the side of their hats and the collar of their jackets; this badge of the 19th Alberta Dragoons, featuring a horse above the unit's designation on a scroll, is that most commonly seen in images. The Canadian Light Horse wore the British jacket with a light blue/scarlet/royal blue slip-on loop for the shoulder strap and brass 'CLH' shoulder titles. Cavalry breeches, puttees, boots with spurs, brown leather bandolier and the M1908 cavalry sword completed the outfit.

G1: Lieutenant-colonel, Canadian Army Medical Corps, c.1917

This figure is based on photos of possibly the best-known medical officer of the Great War, LtCol John McCrae, MD (1872–1918) from Guelph, Ontario. He is shown in the standard British officer's khaki SD uniform with cuff ranking; the CAMC badge was worn on his cap only. McCrae was a fine doctor, a sensitive man and a talented poet.

A rare back view of the Canadian Army Medical Corps nursing sister's ward uniform (see Plate G2), in a detail from a 1918 painting by Gerald Edward Moira of No.3 Stationary Hospital at Doullens, near Amiens. The white veil and apron are worn with the light blue dress; stockings and shoes are black. In total, Canadian hospitals maintained some 13,500 beds in various war zones. (Canadian War Museum, Ottawa)

In May 1915 he wrote 'In Flanders Fields', one of the defining poems of the Great War; the poppies worn by countless individuals in many countries every 11 November are due to his famous verses, beginning:

In Flanders fields the poppies blow
Between the crosses, row on row …

On 28 January 1918 LtCol McCrae died of pneumonia and meningitis. Before he died he had the satisfaction of knowing that his poem had been an outstanding success. It was translated into many languages, and used on billboards advertising the sale of the first Victory Loan Bonds in Canada in 1917; expected to raise $150 million, the campaign raised $400 million.

G2 & 3: Canadian Army Medical Corps nursing sisters, 1914–19

The CAMC nurses wore a light blue dress, which gave rise to the affectionate nickname 'the bluebirds' from grateful CEF personnel who came under their care. The hue of the dresses varied – they could also be a light blue-grey – and they were trimmed with brass buttons in lancer style. The walking-out uniform worn over the dress was a dark blue double-breasted overcoat lined with red, with deep cuffs; all CAMC nurses held officer's commissions, and their shoulder straps bore the 'pips' of their rank. It was worn with a broad dark blue felt hat with the CAMC badge. The veil, dress cuffs, collar, blouse and the apron worn with ward dress were white, and the uniform was completed by a brown leather belt, black stockings and shoes. Nurses also had a grey smock and, for those doing duty in operating rooms, an all-white uniform and head covering. (Uniforms and art at the Canadian War Museum, Ottawa, and period photos, notably the Canadian Letters and Images Project, Malaspina University College and University of Western Ontario)

H: AIR & NAVAL SERVICES

Nearly 23,000 Canadians joined the British Royal Flying Corps and Royal Naval Air Service, of whom some 1,560 died. Of 65 British and Empire pilots who shot down more than 20 enemy aircraft, 12 were Canadians. The leading surviving British and Empire 'ace' was LtCol W.A.'Billy' Bishop, VC, DSO**, MC* (72 confirmed kills); the third was LtCdr Raymond Collishaw, DSO*, DFC, DSC (with 60).

The Royal Canadian Navy grew from some 350 all ranks and a handful of vessels in 1914, to over 100 vessels and 5,500 personnel in 1918; more than 3,000 others served in the Royal Navy. The RCN patrolled both Atlantic and Pacific coasts, but its major contribution was to the war against German U-boats.

Rear Admiral Sir Charles Kingsmill, flag officer commanding the Royal Canadian Navy, c.1915. Sir Charles is shown in the 'undress' dark blue uniform with gold buttons and lace, as usually worn for most duties. A white summer cover is added to the dark blue crown of the peaked (visored) cap, which has a black lace band and a patent leather peak with gold foliate embroidery of rank. The badge is the Royal Navy's silver anchor set in a crowned gold wreath. (Dept of National Defence, History & Heritage Directorate, Ottawa)

H1: Pilot, Royal Flying Corps, 1917–18

No uniform distinction was worn before August 1918, when a curved 'CANADA' shoulder title was added, in gold on khaki for officers and red on khaki for other ranks (in the RNAS, in gold and pale blue respectively, on black). Like all nationalities, aircrew dressed to face the cold in open cockpits, in a variety of issued and privately purchased flying gear. The head is protected here by a soft leather helmet, the face by a fur-lined mask and goggles. This full-length flying coat is made of rubberized canvas lined with goatskin and has a large sheepskin collar. The fleece-lined gauntlet mittens have separate thumbs and forefingers to allow operation of controls and guns. Sheepskin-lined thigh boots were introduced in 1917, as planes now flew higher into colder air that made earlier footwear unsuitable. Many pilots carried pistols; for instance, Lloyd Breadner had a 1911 Colt with a specially adapted holster. (Canadian War Museum, Ottawa)

H2: Seaman, Royal Canadian Navy, 1914–18

The uniforms worn by enlisted men in the RCN were similar in almost every respect to those of Britain's Royal Navy. The Canadian distinction for the ratings was seen on the black cap tally, with the gold letters 'H.M.C.S.' – for 'His Majesty's Canadian Ship' — followed by the name of the ship, e.g. 'Rainbow' or 'Niobe'. From 1916 Canadian vessels were largely deployed on North Atlantic patrols, and the following year a 'warm clothing issue' was approved for these crews. This consisted of a 'winter cap or balaclava helmet', mitts, a jersey, a comforter, thick stockings, wool drawers and thick socks. Engine-room ratings had two flannel vests and petty officers had a cardigan waistcoat instead of a jersey. (*Canadian Naval Orders 1912–1919*, Ottawa, 1919)

H3: Lieutenant, Royal Naval Canadian Volunteer Reserve, 1914–18

The RCN officers' uniforms were exactly the same as those of the RN, and even their crown-and-anchor buttons did not bear the word 'Canada' until the 1920s. In 1917, however, officers were allowed to have their undress uniforms made of blue serge for warm weather. The members of the RNCVR had similar uniforms to those of the Royal Naval Volunteer Reserve, which were identical to those of the RN except that the officer's gold rank lace was set in undulating 'wavy' bands on the cuffs and shoulder straps. The rating's cap ribbons bore 'R.N.C.V.R. [crown] ATLANTIC', 'R.N.C.V.R. [crown] CENTRAL', and 'R.N.C.V.R. [crown] PACIFIC' for the naval reserve's three regions. They did not display individual ship's names.

INDEX

Figures in **bold** refer to illustrations.